T5-CVG-199

THE GUIDE TO INTERNET JOB SEARCHING

Margaret Riley ■ Frances Roehm ■ Steve Oserman

Job and Career Information Services
Committee of the Adult
Lifelong Learning Section

Public Library Association
American Library Association

Printed on recyclable paper

VGM Career Horizons
a division of *NTC Publishing Group*
Lincolnwood, Illinois USA

Library of Congress Cataloging-in-Publication Data
Riley, Margaret.
The guide to Internet job searching / Margaret Riley, Frances Roehm, Steve Oserman.
p. cm.
"Job and Career Information Services Committee of the Adult Lifelong Learning Section, Public Library Association, American Library Association."
Includes bibliographical references and index.
ISBN 0-8442-8197-2 (pbk.)
1. Job hunting—Computer network resources. 2. Internet (Computer network) 3. World Wide Web (Information retrieval system)
I. Roehm, Frances E. II. Oserman, Steve. III. Public Library Association. Job and Career Information Services Committe.
IV. Title.
HF5382 . 7 . R557 1996
025 . 06 ' 65014—dc20 96-1785
CIP

"Harry's Job Search BBS & Internet Hot List" used by kind permission of Harry Lemon. © 1995 by Harold Lemon.

Published by VGM Career Horizons, a division of NTC Publishing Group
4255 West Touhy Avenue
Lincolnwood (Chicago), Illinois 60646-1975, U.S.A.
© 1996 by The Public Library Association/American Library Association.
All rights reserved. No part of this book may be reproduced, stored in a retrieval system, or transmitted in any form or by any means, electronic, mechanical, photocopying, recording, or otherwise, without the prior permission of NTC Publishing Group.
Manufactured in the United States of America.

67890 VL 98765432

Contents

Preface

Our local communities are adapting to the rapid changes in communication technology: schools, local governments, libraries, businesses, and other groups are receiving and distributing information via the Internet. Today's public libraries are playing a vital role in the development of these local initiatives, and many of them are offering a connection with the information sources on the Internet along with their more traditional services.

The World Wide Web and its easy-to-use browsing and searching features has encouraged this rapid adaptation to Internet information services. Traditional information providers are finding that these services are not only "user friendly," but also cost effective—saving paper, staff time, and long-distance charges—essentially, getting more bang for the buck.

Job and career information is perfectly suited to the trend toward online services, and the growth in Internet resources and services in this area is skyrocketing. In electronic format, information can be accessed from anywhere and by anyone on the planet! Job postings can be keyed or scanned in very quickly, making the information available almost as soon as a position is open. Résumés can be matched to companies or suitable job listings. Potential employees can obtain information about a company prior to the interview.

Public libraries have traditionally played a vital role in the job search, providing local and national newspapers, career guides, and knowledge of the community and its agencies to direct individuals to the information they need. With the changing job scene and the increasing number of electronic career services online, on the Internet, and on CD-ROM, your public library is more important than ever!

This PLA Guide will show you how to access necessary information and where to look for it. It will also give you the guidelines you need to manage this new, more active environment. Your public library can help point the way with books about the job search, writing résumés, and other career guides, as well as the new materials on using the Internet. If it doesn't already, it also may soon provide you with access to the Internet. If you live in a community whose public library doesn't provide these services yet, try the local community college or high school. In any event, we hope it's just a matter of time until you can be surfing with the best of them, adding a new dimension to your job search with great results.

Use the guide with our best wishes for success in your job search!

Frances E. Roehm
Bloomington, IL

Margaret F. Riley
Reston, VA

Acknowledgments

We have many people to thank for their assistance and support in producing the book you hold in your hands. These people were instrumental in our efforts by helping to evaluate thousands of Internet resources and to make the final selection of the hundreds included here. You can see what a diverse group of people worked on this project. A true Internet endeavor!

- Steve Oserman, Adult Reference Services and Career Services, Skokie Public Library, IL. Co-chair of the JCIS committee of the PLA, and the brains behind this whole thing.
- Deborah Wright, cataloger, Gordon Library, Worcester Polytechnic Institute, MA.
- Harold Lemon, computer consultant and author of *Harry's List of Dial-up BBS*, Union City, CA.
- Frank Fessenden, Director, Hiatt Career Center, Brandeis University, MA.
- Janine Harig, Career and Life Planning Center, Johns Hopkins University, MD.
- Jane Stein, Assistant Director, Career Planning and Placement, Texas A&M University—Corpus Christie, TX.
- Brian Ryan, The Logan Group, Executive Search Consultants, St. Louis, MO.
- Gerald T. Crispin, SPHR, National Employment Practices Committee, Society for Human Resource Management and VP, Shaker Advertising, NJ.
- Jon Ishihara, Career Counselor, Career Services, University of Hawaii at Manoa, HI.
- Sandra J. Erickson, Senior Computer Support Specialist and Career Service staff member, University of South Dakota, SD.
- Elizabeth A. Lorenzen, Career Center Librarian, Indiana State University Libraries, IN.

We owe a great deal to those who agreed to be interviewed for Appendix A:

- Marcia Fawcett, principal of The Fawcett Group, North Grafton, MA.
- Dr. Laurence J. Stybel, president of Stybel Peabody/ Lincolnshire, Boston, MA.

- Kathleen Bovard, Director of the Career and Life Planning Center, School of Continuing Studies, Johns Hopkins University, MD.

We are also grateful to those who contributed the job search tips that are featured at the beginning of the resource chapters. Their names are listed with their contributions.

On a more personal note, we'd each like to thank those who have supported us not only in this project but in many other areas as well.

From Frances:
In memory of my parents, Louis B. and Mary Kathryn Sutton.

And my thanks to those who continue to make my life easier—
Leonard J. Cotter, for his patience and great pastries;
My son, Christopher Roehm, for his enthusiastic support;
and Rao Duvvuri, for his technical assistance.

From Margaret:
This book is dedicated to all of those who have helped guide me and support me throughout my life:

My parents, Stewart and Marian Finkler, and my family, who have always been there.

My buddies who pushed me forward and kept the chocolate coming during the tough times, including Brad Taylor, Hilde Horvath, Lou Rosenfeld, Harold, and Debbie.

The many friends and colleagues I've met in my work with job and career resources and who have taught me a lot more than I realized I needed to know, including Nicholas Rench, Frank, Marcy, the career services staff at WPI, and everyone on JobPlace.

The librarians who have influenced not only my choice of career but my professional ideals and dedication to them, including Reg Didham, David Ferriero, Jerry Miller, and A.J. Anderson.

The students at WPI who were the reason I started this all. Necessity really is the mother of invention.

Very special thanks to Joyce Lain Kennedy for her advice and assistance and to the many others who have offered their advice and assistance to this project.

Foreword

Welcome to the World of Possibility

If you haven't yet donned your career search equipment, leapt on your surfboard and skimmed through the vast, maze-like corridors, channels, and landing sites of the global Internet, you're in for a treat.

If you set off on the journey through this multitude of multiplicity without a guide, you're in for confusion and frustration as well. And since you are holding this book in your hands, you probably already know that Margaret F. Riley is quite a guide. Her knowledge and understanding of how to master the complexities of the network career search are encyclopedic. She shows you not only how to surf, but also where the surf is running best; where the waves and currents can give you a great ride without too many spills.

In this book, you will get a double helping of benefit. Not only are you going to discover new ways to manage your career and job search, you're also going to build a skill that is becoming more and more relevant in all areas of work: how to interact with the Global International Network of information fondly known as The Net.

The Hidden Job Market Revealed

It has been our contention for decades that the people who get the best opportunities and cash in on the best job openings are those who step outside the customary channels of help-wanted advertising into the world of proactive "find what you want—don't just take what's handed to you." Since most jobs are not advertised on any given day and are disseminated by word of mouth, chance referrals, and insider information, those who are most able to initiate contact, open new sources of information, and communicate clearly about what they want rather than hoping to find what's available are most successful.

In the past, exploring the hidden job market meant trips to the library, mail-list research, hundreds of phone calls, composing cover letters and résumés, and running what looked like a small direct mail service out of the basement. All that has changed, and is changing, as the World Wide Web (WWW) continues to multiply, diversify, and become ever more accessible to the average person with a computer and a modem.

This global network has some interesting features to consider from a career search prospective: all the information is there *waiting* to be accessed. With very few exceptions you are invited to surf in these waters to your heart's content. This gateway is open to you 24 hours a day, 365 days a year, across 24 time zones. If you are a midnight voyager, all lines are open. If you choose to do your career shopping on New Year's Eve, no problem. Unlike the local library, the Internet offers two-, three-, and multiple-way communication both into the networks (sending messages) as well as taking the information away. Virtually every resource station, Web page, forum, or newsnet station are open for messages from you to them as well as from them to you. And much of it is free.

Traditional networking before the cyber-revolution meant cold calling people you might have known only vaguely, perhaps having to get beyond secretarial gatekeepers, and then having 30 seconds to plead your need for a referral or reference or whatever. The strength of this type of networking was that you often built up good personal connections with a few select people who knew some or all of the answers you needed.

The Internet is, on the face of it at least, less personal: you are invited to make inquiries, send messages, present your information, and follow up using short, communicator language with little personality. Perhaps it's not so impersonal as was once thought, however. For some, the brevity protocol is a blessing. Make your point and move on. There is little of the fear that goes with cold calling, no "out to lunch" signs, and few gatekeepers. (Even Bill Gates does his own e-mail!) And you won't run out of contacts.

In fact, there might be too much information available—too many sites, too many connections, and, finally, too many thousands of people surfing in the same ocean to get the same warm and fuzzy feeling of comfort you do from the people in your personal at-home network you know are "yours." Knowing the rules of each approach in advance is one of the most important keys to mastering the Internet career search.

If you accept the idea of the Internet as an interactive hidden job market, you will realize that capturing the career or job you're interested in is not simply a matter of gaining the information and the contacts. It's still about making the kind of presentation that answers that fundamental question: "why should I hire you?" This is not going to go away no matter how powerful the computers and how varied the Web sites.

To the degree that the Internet is a kind of information free-for-all you need to avoid getting caught up in the melee and step back to strategize how to make the most compelling case for what you offer to potential employers—in Netspeak—so they find you interesting and worth interviewing and hiring. You might even have to make a more compelling case than you would through normal channels because of the number of inquiries organizations are receiving from others due to the very nature of their wide global reach.

Becoming Indelible

Presenting yourself effectively on the Internet and its nodes takes on a different complexity than the conventional means you are used to. The Internet is made up of people connecting. How many are out there who are experts in a field you are targeting and know what's happening in your field right now? Many, many, many. How do you reach them? Considering that by the time you read this the forthcoming Global Career Link might not yet have been implemented, you will need to use good communications and discretion to make an impact in the various industrially focused sites Margaret talks of so they will be interested in you.

People are quite sensitive to the content of communications on the Internet, as Margaret points out in this book. Getting "flamed" isn't the best way to establish a meaningful relationship, and that can and does happen if you don't know the rules—written and unwritten—that are growing within this global subculture.

Internetting is not all that different from traditional networking in that as you contact someone new you want to be very careful about not wasting their time or coming across as a sort of "charity case." Oftentimes a simple question posted on the right bulletin board will yield great dividends. A person we know received an offer from a company that did not provide employee benefits. The recruiter said they had raised the salary offered by 15 percent in order to compensate for this. The job seeker, not knowing whether this was a good deal or not, posted the question with one of the forums. Within a few days a response came through from a recently retired senior compensation expert who was happy to provide as much inside scoop as he could. Score another one for the Internet!

Having used the Internet for (1) making a fast sweep into the hidden job market and identifying scores of organizations that could be potential future employers; and (2) getting inside information about the kind of presentation you need to make from individuals with that experience, you can move to the third benefit of the Internet: a full education about how to manage your career search. There are already several career counseling modalities on the Internet. Margaret describes these quite well in Appendix C. Some of them—like Mainstream Online on the Microsoft Network—provide counseling and job-search tools for a small fee to cover the cost of the professional materials offered, and others will provide you with more informatal interactions at no fee. Trust Margaret to have the answers for this.

Happy hunting. You are entering a world being birthed before your very eyes: a new continent arising out of a familiar ocean. There is a steep learning curve that no expert or authority can give you; it's about learning as you go, testing and trying new approaches, and stretching your imagination as far and wide as this unique and revolutionary communication universe will let you.

Surf on!

Tom Jackson

CHAPTER 1

Using the Internet in Your Job Search

What Is the Internet Job Search?

You can find any number of books about job hunting and about the Internet. Why is the Internet so important to the job search, and why do you need a book about it? You can just get on the Web and get everything, right? *Wrong*! Job hunting on the Internet uses a broad variety of information networks and resources. No single list, network, or resource will contain all of the information you want or need. To use the Internet effectively in your job search, you must be prepared to look at every piece of it:

- Usenet newsgroups
- Mailing lists
- Electronic journals
- Telnet sites
- Gopher servers
- World Wide Web servers

You might be able to pick and choose among these Internet services to better customize your search, but they are all essential pieces of your strategy.

Why Use the Internet?

Many of you are sitting out there wondering why you picked up this book. The job search is already tough. Why do you want to make it any harder by looking at something as vast as the Internet? There are several reasons the Internet can be an asset to your job search.

1. **Networking !** Experts suggest that 80 percent of available jobs are never advertised. They are filled by a friend or acquaintance of someone already in the organization or by persons already known to the organization. All of the job gurus say that networking is an important part of making the job search a success. The Internet is the world's largest network, so use its reach to your advantage. Get to know people both near and far, because sometimes those distant contacts can be much closer than you think.
2. **Current growth of online job listings.** As the Internet grows and expands, so do the number of participants and

the resources for finding jobs. Profit and nonprofit organizations are coming online, and they are finding it easy and inexpensive to add their job openings to their public servers. These organizations are also posting their jobs on networks and services set up to recruit new employees. To gain access to all of these opportunities, you need to be online too.

3. **Round-the-clock availability.** Many job seekers cannot search for work during regular business hours because of current work schedules or other responsibilities. The Internet is available to you when you are ready to use it, 24 hours a day, seven days a week, regardless of time zones. Employers aren't concerned that you are looking for job opportunities at 2 A.M., they are only concerned with finding the best person to fill their position. If your letter and résumé will be accepted via e-mail, they can be sent at any time and be waiting in an e-mail box for the first person who comes in the next morning.
4. **Free access to information and resources.** Once you have access to the Internet, you can access hundreds of free resources for job listings, help in writing résumés and constructing cover letters, and even planning your career path online. While several agencies in your community can help you in the same ways, many of them are limited in their hours of operation. Consult your local agencies and use their support and feedback, but also use the good resources you find online, again with that 24-hour access!
5. **Broad geographic reach.** Current employment trends in the United States and abroad are making us a more mobile society. Perhaps your spouse or companion has been transferred, or you just want to move elsewhere to try for better or different work. You can begin investigating that move now on the Internet. Use it to check out various cities and regions. You can even look at other countries, find out what opportunities for employment exist there, and begin contacting employers. You may be able to set up interviews by phone or have them scheduled for shortly after your arrival. If you are moving across the state, across the country, or out of the country, there is no need to wait until you actually arrive in your new location to begin your search for employment.
6. **Opportunity to demonstrate skills.** Organizations, espe-cially businesses, are rushing to get onto the Internet. They see opportunities for advertising, possible commercial mar-kets, and a vast wealth of information they can tap. Your Internet job search demonstrates to an employer your familiarity and skill with this new market area, and that could set you apart from other candidates. If you found the job information on the Internet, make sure you let the employer know this.

7. **The ease of keywords.*** How many newspapers do you read to look for employment? Think of each newspaper as a separate database of information. You read the classified ads of each one looking for job titles, lists of required skills, and position responsibilities that match your own interests and experiences. Unless your newspaper uses keywords to bring all job listings in a field together, you have to read the entire help wanted section to find all of the possible listings in your field, and even then you may miss some. A job in human resource management may be listed under "Personnel," "Human Resources," or even "Employee Administration," but the skills and responsibilities are consistent. Keyword searching in the various Internet databases and resources allows you to pull up similar listings much more quickly and efficiently, cutting down on the amount of time and effort you need to put into each separate database.
8. **Tips on companies that are increasing staffing.*** You see a company's job listings online, and you wonder if it has any openings of interest to you. Check the public Internet server to see for yourself, but also think about contacting the company even if your specific area is not being recruited at this time. Indicate in your cover letter that you noticed positions were available, and tell how your area of expertise can be of use. Be a step ahead and the first in line with a résumé when those hiring turn their attention toward your field.
9. **Résumé posting at no cost.*** There are several databases and newsgroups that allow you to post your résumé at no charge once you have Internet access. Although this raises some questions about your control over and the confidentiality of your résumé, it is an effective way to get your résumé seen by recruiters and employers who use these databases regularly.

Job Search Tip: The Internet is not just for techies anymore! As the number of participants grows, so does the diversity of online information and job listings. Move away from the **misc. jobs.offered** newsgroup and follow the smaller newgroups discussing topics in your field. Look for links to more specific information resources for other good starting points.

* Goldsborough, Reid. *Straight Talk About the Information Superhighway.* Alpha Books, 1994, p. 48.

Getting Started on the Internet: Connectivity and the Basics

Before we take you onto the Internet to begin your job search, we'll take a few minutes to talk about what you are about to get into. Almost every general Internet book gives you an overview of the Internet and a bit of its history, so we'll skip that. You can also pick up any number of good books on how to use the Internet at your local public library. At the end of this chapter we have listed those we find most useful, along with some great magazines to help you online. What we will address in this chapter is how you can connect to the Internet, the places you might be able to hook up, and the equipment you will need to use all the pieces of the Internet.

"*All* the pieces?" Yes, *all* the pieces. The Internet is a mix of networks and computers with different ways of connecting and communicating, called *protocols*. To use the Internet effectively for your job search means learning enough about these networks and the various ways of communicating to find the information you need.

What do you need to learn in order to use the Internet? You need to learn how to connect to computers using Telnet and file transfer protocol (FTP). You need to learn how to communicate using electronic (e-mail) mailing lists, and Usenet newsgroups. You also need to know about the networks for accessing both Gopher and World Wide Web servers. If you don't have access to Gopher and the Web, you can telnet to public Gopher and Web servers.

In addition to the various Internet networks, connectors, and communication protocols, there are several different software programs to access each piece, so you may find yourself looking at one program at home but a different one at work or at the library. The thing to remember is that all of these programs have the same basic functions, so if you can't find a book that discusses the program you have access to, use the ideas and functions outlined in another book and look for similar features in your program. Several important features will always be present, no matter which software program you use.

Internet Tip: Although there are several programs to access the various parts of the Internet, they are grouped into basic categories.

- *Mailers* are those programs you use to read and send e-mail.
- *Newsreaders* are used to read the Usenet newsgroups.
- *Web browsers* are used to access the World Wide Web, and they can also be used to access Gopher servers. Some of these are text based, but many will display graphics.

Equipment Needed to Use the Internet

Do you have a computer with a hard drive, a 2400 baud modem, and a communication program? If so, you are all set to go online. That is all you need to access the Internet. You don't really need high-speed modems, Windows, graphics capability, or color monitors unless you want to use a graphical browser to access the World Wide Web. You just need something reliable to dial into the provider's service and display the text. You'll want a printer too, so you can print the things you find online, especially the job listings, but even this doesn't have to be fancy. It just all needs to be reliable.

What if you don't have a computer but are willing to buy one? You can decide for yourself between a PC and a Macintosh system, either will work. Regardless of the system you decide to buy, keep these few ideas in mind when you are computer shopping.

1. **Speed.** Get the fastest processor and the fastest modem you can afford. Processor speeds are measured in *megahertz* (MHz), and modem speeds are measured in *bits per second* (bps), also referred to as *baud rates*. The higher the numbers, the faster the equipment.
2. **Memory.** Get the biggest hard drive and the most *random access memory* (RAM) you can. Memory is measured in *bytes*, and the amounts found in personal computers are stated in terms of *kilobytes* (K) or *megabytes* (MB). If you get a new computer, look for a 500 MB hard drive and at least 4MB of RAM; 8MB of RAM would be even better.
3. **A good monitor.** Your eyes are important, and using a computer can be strenuous on your eyes, especially after a long day at work. Get the best monitor you can afford. Ask about the *resolution* or clarity. The higher the numbers, the better the monitor. Also ask about the *pitch*, the space between the letters. The smaller the numbers, the better.

You might be able to get a used computer at a great bargain. Check the newspaper for people selling their old computers, watch for "computer swap" meets, or see if there is a computer-user club in your area. Members might be able to help you get set up for a low price. Then you will be ready to surf the Internet with the rest of the world! Oh, wait. There is one more thing. You'll need an account somewhere for access to the Internet.

Internet Tip: If you want to view the graphics on the World Wide Web, you will need a 486 PC with Windows 3.1 or higher and a modem that connects at 14400 bps or faster. For Macintosh users, you should have Mac System 7 or later.

When you call providers about access through their services, ask them what software you need in order to use their **graphical browser** for the Web.

Connecting to the Internet

Several places make it possible for you to access the Internet. Some of these will charge you, but you may be lucky enough to live in an area that provides free Internet access. Here is a list of the places to check for Internet access, starting with some free sources.

1. **Your public library.** Many public libraries are getting funding from government agencies or local companies to set up public terminals with Internet access. Eugene, OR; Seattle, WA; and Cambridge, MA are just three communities that offer this service, and many others will be joining them soon.
2. **Community freenets.** Many local networks are forming to provide information on communities, their governments, and local businesses, and these networks are also connecting to the Internet. Check with your public library or a computer user group to see if one is available in your area.
3. **Your place of work.** More organizations and businesses are joining the Internet, and many permit their employees to access it also. If they do, there may be in-house regulations for use and security precautions. Check with your employer.
4. **Cybercafes.** Believe it or not, there are new businesses opening that give you a place to go for a sandwich, a cup of coffee, and an Internet connection. CyberSmith in Cambridge, MA, is one of these. You buy a card with some cash credit on it and pay for the amount of time you are connected.

5. **Commercial providers.** America Online, CompuServe, Prodigy, and many other similar services all offer some access to the Internet. You can send e-mail to the Internet, read Usenet newsgroups, and use a *Web browser* to access the World Wide Web and Gopher. However, these providers might not offer Telnet and FTP access.
6. **Internet access providers,** also called Internet service providers. Like the commercial providers, you pay a monthly fee and are given a software package to use when connecting, but these services connect you directly to the Internet and give you full access to e-mail, Telnet, FTP, Usenet newsgroups, Gopher, and the Web.

Internet Tip: What is the difference between using a commercial provider like Prodigy and an Internet access provider? It depends on what you want. Prodigy and the other commercial providers have a great deal of information within their private networks that Internet users cannot get to. These private networks are usually well organized and the information is easy to find, an advantage of which the Internet cannot boast. On the other hand, some commercial providers charge you an extra fee to connect to the Internet through them, and a lot of the information they have can be duplicated on the Internet once you learn the ins and outs. The final decision is yours.

If you are one of those lucky people with several options for Internet access, how do you select the best one for you? Is it always best to use a free service? No, not always. Your public library may not be able to give you an e-mail account, and cybercafés probably won't let you register for e-mail either. Your community freenet might be so busy you can't get connected. Many employers only allow e-mail access for their employees. You may already be thinking about buying an account either through a commercial provider, such as CompuServe, or a full-service Internet access provider, so how do you go about deciding which service has the best deal for you? Here are some questions to ask the services and providers you contact.

1. **How much will it cost?** If there is a fee, what is the *set-up fee* (*the original cost to get you started*) and the *usage fee* (*the monthly base charge*)? What do these include? Is there a *fee for connect time* (*the actual amount of time you spend online*)? How are these charges **collected**? Some companies want your credit card number to keep on file.
2. **Is there a local number you can dial to access the service?** You don't want to pay long-distance charges for

access. Ask for a complete list of their dial-in numbers and check them yourself.

3. **What Internet services will you have access to?** For your job search, the minimum you need is e-mail, Telnet capability, and access to Usenet newsgroups. Additional access to a Web browser is ideal. (*The Web browser can be used to access Gopher servers.*) You can use Telnet to reach public Gopher and Web clients, but the integrated package is better and will give you more flexibility.
4. **What computers and operating systems do they support?** Can you get software that runs on DOS or Macintosh? Do you need Windows 3.1 or higher? Can you get a package that will work with your OS/2 system? Tell them what you have right now and see if they can handle it.
5. **Do they supply software that enables you to read and respond to news and e-mail offline?** If you are paying connect fees, this software can save you a lot of time and money.
6. **What are their minimum and maximum baud rates for connecting?** At the very least, they should offer connectivity from **2400 to 14400 bps**. Some services no longer support 1200 bps connections, but not everyone supports the higher speeds either.
7. **Is there an additional cost for the higher connect speeds?** Will they charge you extra to connect at 14400 or 28800 bps?
8. **What is their modem-to-user ratio?** Find out how easy it will be to connect when you want to. A ratio of *30-to-1* may mean that you will get a lot of busy signals. A ratio of *15-to-1* is much more reasonable.
9. **How do you get help if you get stuck?** Does the provider have a local or 800 number to call, and will they respond to your calls? At what times can you get support—during working hours only, or is help available late evenings and weekends too? Also, ask how large their support staff is. Only one person is not enough, even during low-use periods.
10. **Can you get some free time to try their service?** Most providers will let you try them out for five hours or so at no cost. Go ahead and ask!

Call several providers and ask these questions. Then compare their answers. Online access is becoming a competitive business, so shop around for the best rates, the best deals, and the package that best fits your needs.

More Recommended Reading about the Internet

Check your local library for these titles. If it doesn't have them in its collection, ask the librarians if they can get them for you via interlibrary loan or if they might recommend other good titles.

Books

- Dern, Daniel P. *The Internet Guide for New Users*. New York: McGraw-Hill, 1994.
- Gilster, Paul. *The Internet Navigator*, 2nd ed. New York: Wiley, 1994. (Anything by this author is good for all user levels.)
- Hahn, Harley. *The Internet Complete Reference*. Berkeley, CA: Osbourne McGraw-Hill, 1994.
- Harrison, Mark. *The Usenet Handbook: A User's Guide to Netnews*. Sebastopol, CA: O'Reilly, 1995.
- Kehoe, Brendan P. *Zen and the Art of the Internet: A Beginner's Guide*, 2nd ed. Englewood Cliffs, NJ: PTR Prentice Hall, 1993.
- Krol, Ed. *The Whole Internet User's Guide & Catalog*, 2nd ed. Sebastopol, CA: O'Reilly, 1994. (This is better for those who are more computer literate.)
- Levine, John R, and Carol Baroudi. *Internet for Dummies*, 2nd ed. San Mateo, CA: IDG, 1994. (This title is highly recommended for the computer fearful.)
- Smith, Richard J., and Mak Gibbs. *Navigating the Internet*, Deluxe ed. Indianapolis, IN: Sams, 1994.

Magazines (Subscription Information)

Computer Currents
Computer Currents Publishing, Inc.
5720 Hollis St., Emeryville, CA 94608
Phone: (510) 547-6800.

Internet World
U.S. and Canada:
MecklerMedia Corp, P.O. Box 713,
Mount Morris, IL 61054-9965
Phone: (800) 573-3062
Elsewhere:
Mecklermedia Ltd., Artillery House, Artillery Row,
London SWIP 1RT, England

Phone: (0171) 976-0405

NetGuide
CMP Media
P.O. Box 420355, Palm Coast, FL 32142-9371
Phone: (800) 829-0421

Wired
Wired Ventures, Inc
P.O.Box 191826, San Francisco, CA 94119-9866
Phone: (800) SO WIRED (U.S. only)
Phone: (415) 222-6200

CHAPTER 2

The Internet Job Application

You know why you want to go online, you know how to get online, you think you know what you are getting yourself into, so let's go! *Wait a second!* First things first. How do you *respond* to the job listings you find on the Internet? Do you just send e-mail back to the poster and say, "Hi, I want that job you advertised on the Internet?" *No!* Your electronic employment application has to be just as good online as it is off, so let's take a minute to go over a few more things before you begin your electronic job search.

Applying for Positions Advertised on the Internet

The fastest way to respond to Internet job listings is by e-mailing your cover letter and résumé to the person or agency indicated. You still need a great résumé and fantastic cover letter, but they will be handled a little differently.

1. **Have a résumé prepared and stored in text format, sometimes called ASCII or DOS text, for sending via e-mail**. (*See* "Preparing Your Résumé for E-mail.") Check it and make sure it looks good! You don't want your text to wrap and look bad on a different size screen, so keep the width to *70 columns (characters) wide*. Absolutely no word processing or PostScript files! These will not e-mail well, and the person on the receiving end will not want to take the time to make your résumé look good again.
2. **Include a cover letter and be sure to note where you found the ad.** Make sure the company knows you are an Internet user and that their online recruiting has been successful so they will do it again. You can create and store a "standard" cover letter in text, but remember to customize it for each job listing you are applying for. Again, check the format and width before you send it.
3. **Send your résumé and cover letter in one file.** Would you mail a letter and résumé in separate envelopes? *Never!* You may think your résumé is too long because it covers many screens, but if you have written a one- or two-page résumé and merely transferred it, it is the proper length. Catch the employer's eye with a good objective statement and a summary of your skills at the top.
4. **Use the job title that was advertised as your "Subject" line in the e-mail, citing any relevant job numbers as noted in the ad.** This makes it easy to route your résumé and letter to the appropriate person.

If you are "cold calling" to get your résumé into someone's hands without referencing an advertised position, put a few words stating your objective in the "Subject" line. If you use one Internet job service frequently and have had good luck finding positions advertised there, consider registering your résumé with that service. Then you can send a message with the reference number of your résumé to apply for any position that service advertises.

5. ***Warning:* Some employers who advertise online do not accept résumés via e-mail!** Sometimes employers want the materials sent to a different e-mail address, but sometimes they will only accept résumés via fax or regular mail. Be sure to read a listing carefully before you respond to it! Follow the directions for applications as the company has given them. You don't want to send your résumé to the wrong address or the wrong person. Always cite the job title advertised and any code numbers they request.

> **Job Search Tip:** It is very important that you read the *entire* posting and respond according to the directions given. It only takes a second and a couple of keystrokes to delete a message that wasn't sent properly, and you don't want that to happen to you. *Read and think before you respond!*

Preparing Your Résumé for E-Mail

This is not difficult. Most word processors and résumé-writing programs will let you save a file to *plain text*, also called **DOS** or **ASCII text**.

1. Create your résumé using the formatting and display style recommended by the people helping you or the guides you are reading. Check it for spelling and grammar, and read it over carefully to be sure you find any mistakes the computer didn't.
2. Print a copy of the résumé, make a copy of the computer file, naming it **résumé.txt**, and tell the program to save this to text.
3. Using any **text editor**, even your word processor, edit the **résumé.txt** file to resemble your printed résumé.

Notepad in the Windows program is one example of a text editor. Redo the spacing using the space bar, and add some unique characters to highlight your skills, and so on, just like you did before. Remember that you may need to alter the margins a bit for the e-mail. Save this copy as text!

4. Save both copies of the files on a diskette so your résumé is ready to edit, print, or e-mail on demand.

Internet Tip: Highlighting Your Résumé. Since you cannot use boldface, underscoring, or bullets in a plain text document, consider using the following characters as substitutes:

- Try *asterisks* (*) or *plus signs* (+) instead of bullets at the beginning of lines.
- Use a *series of dashes* to separate sections. Don't try to underline text.
- Consider using *capital letters* to replace bold type, or use *asterisks* to surround the text. Don't try to highlight text within your résumé, but highlight the headers or titles of each section.

Once you have redone your résumé in the text format, send it to yourself or to a friend to see how it looks after it is e-mailed.

There are several places on the Internet where you can examine text résumés to see what other job seekers have done to present their information. The **misc.jobs.resumes** Usenet newsgroup is one good place to view résumés. **Career Magazine** (*http://www.careermag.com/careermag*) has a résumé database on its webserver that you can search. You will see some very good and not so good ideas.

Posting Your Résumé

For some people, posting a résumé has been a great way to get work. For others, there is the fear that someone they don't know will get their home address and phone number; still others don't want some people or organizations looking at their résumés. Control and confidentiality might be a concern for you, so here are some things to think about before posting.

1. **Do you want your résumé made public?** Once you have posted it, consider your résumé a public document and out of your control. Anyone can look in the public databases and see what is there. Even closed résumé databanks do not let you dictate who can and cannot look at your résumé. If possible, consider posting your *skill set*, a summary of your areas of interest and expertise. Instead of putting your home address on the résumé, list just a phone number and e-mail address, if you have one. Many employers and recruiters still prefer to contact you by phone, so if you don't include a phone number, you may be overlooked. If you don't want your home phone number listed, ask a friend or the agency helping you if you can use their number as a contact. Just remember to check for messages!
2. **Check the confidentiality of the database or service where you are placing your résumé.** Who can get access to this database? How is that access granted? Will you be notified if your résumé is forwarded to an employer? Is it possible your boss will see your résumé? If the answers to these questions make you the least bit uncomfortable, consider another service or consider not posting.
3. **Once your résumé is listed, can it be updated *at no cost?*** Some Internet services will let you post your résumé free, but they will charge you for updates. You don't want an old résumé out there, and you don't want to pay for updates. You want an unlimited number of updates, even if it is only to correct a typo or to word something a little better. Skip any service that limits or charges for updates.
4. **Will your résumé be deleted from the databank if you don't update it?** You don't want an old résumé out there, and, if you find employment, you don't necessarily want to be getting calls from other employers. A good database will delete your résumé after three to six months if it is not updated.

You see, it's not all that simple. In fact, it's just as hard as a traditional job search. You have to prepare your résumé, your cover letter, and even yourself for this new online environment. Once you've thought all this over and worked everything out, then you are ready for the next step, that step onto the virtual pavement as you begin looking for work.

Recommended Sites for Posting Your Résumé

The following are ***no-cost*** *sites that have a well-established presence with the many employers and recruiters using the Internet as a part of* ***their*** *hunt for new talent. More information and site listings can be found using the many resources in this book.*

Online Career Center
http://www.occ.com
gopher://occ.com

CareerMosaic
http://www.careermosaic.com/cm/

The Monster Board
http://www.monster.com/

misc.jobs.resumes
Usenet newsgroup

World Wide Job Seekers
http://www.cban.com/resume/

Maintained by Andrew Stanley Jones in Canada, World Wide Job Seekers allow résumés to be posted online in 16 categories and can be accessed by employers throughout the world. This service has a built-in search engine for searches by job, industry, and location.

CHAPTER 3

Pounding the Virtual Pavement: Beginning Your Internet Job Search

You have the résumé, you have the equipment, and you are ready to go online and begin your job search. Where do you start and how do you find the jobs—not just any jobs, but those in your field? Here lies the difficulty of the Internet, namely ***finding the information you want***. What is the best way to search for information, and where can you begin? Let's look at some ideas for finding Internet information, strategies for locating employment opportunities and other good information, and some resources at your beck and call to help you in your search.

Locating Internet Information

The Internet is constantly changing. New resources are added, old ones are moved to new locations, and others are deleted on a daily basis. You must develop a repertoire of strategies, skills, and tactics to give you the flexibility to deal with this fluid environment. You must also know how to approach the problem, where to look for a possible answer, and who to talk to if you are not finding what you want easily. Craig Gibson, Head of Library User Education, Washington State University Libraries, has established a set of models to use for finding Internet information.*

1. **Ask an expert via e-mail.** *Best used when an expert will provide special or unusual knowledge that is unavailable elsewhere*. You can also use this if you need an answer quickly and are already a member of the "invisible family" (that is, a regular participant on the Internet). *This is a last resort online!* Although most Internet users are friendly and helpful, they don't want to do your research for you. When you need to ask a question, be prepared to list everywhere that you have already checked for the answer yourself.
2. **Post a question on a discussion list (mailing list or Usenet newsgroup).** *Best used when communal knowledge will yield a fast, reliable answer*. You can use the lists of Usenet newsgroups and mailing lists to find the best place to ask your question. Several are noted in the resources section at the end of this chapter. Many newsgroups also have *frequently asked questions* (FAQ) documents available. Read these before posting your question.

* Gibson, Craig. "Thinking Skills for the Information Highway." *Sixth International Conference on Thinking*, Massachusetts Institute of Technology, July 20, 1994.

> **<u>Internet Tip</u>: Frequently asked questions (FAQS**) are lists of the most commonly asked questions for Usenet newsgroups and mailing lists. Not every group or list has an FAQ, but it is better to look at the archives and see if one exists before you ask your question. A great collection of these can be found at **http://www.cis.ohio-state.edu/hypertext/faq/usenet/index.html.**

3. **Identify notable Internet sites.** *Best used when certain Internet sites have valuable information needed on a recurring basis, offer unique information or resources, are particularly well organized, or have many pointers to other sites.* You can identify your own list of notable sites or "starting points" through personal exploration, Internet guide books, various Internet discussion lists, or some guides already on the Internet. We have included a list of notable resources at the end of this chapter which are great not only for a job search but for finding all kinds of Internet information.
4. **Select and use a resource discovery tool.** *Best used when you don't know or are uncertain of the location and/or availability of information on the Internet. Exploration and luck are more important than efficiency at this point.* **Resource discovery tools** are the search engines and indexers created for the various pieces of the Internet. We have included a number of these in the resource list at the end of the chapter. You cannot use just one and get all of the available information, but you should use a few and then compare your results. You may have some duplication, but you may also find some unique differences.
5. **Select and use an appropriate Internet protocol (Telnet, FTP, and so on).** *Best used when you know information is available at a specific site.* Use printed and online Internet directions and your resource discovery tools to identify sites, logons, path names, so on, and then connect to them.

What Gibson has identified are three basic ways to locate information: **inquiring, browsing,** and **searching**. Whereas *inquiring* can be a quick way of finding information, many times it won't produce the answer you want or need, or there may be no one who can answer your question. There comes a point when ***you*** must be the expert. You are the one who knows what you want and how you want to get there, so you must take control of your search. This is where browsing and searching come in.

Browsing means you start with a very general term and follow paths or links you encounter until you find something interesting or useful. Strategy 3 in the preceding list relies upon the "browse" mode for discovery. *Searching* means you have a specific goal in mind and the terms to describe or define the information you want to locate, and you want to go directly to that information in as straight a path as possible. Strategies 4 and 5 make use of searching and examining print and online directories and resource discovery tools to locate specific items with the least amount of time and effort.

So, how do you apply these three ideas to your job search on the Internet? It depends on your need at the moment.

Inquiring. *Where do I begin? How do I use this? Can anyone help me locate the information I need?*

Ask on a Usenet newsgroup or a mailing list, or ask a librarian or Internet volunteer for help. Some Internet help books may be useful too.

Browsing. *I just want to take a little look around and see what is available. I'm not really ready to jump in yet.*

Begin with a broad term such as "employment," choose a starting point from the list of virtual libraries and online guides, and follow links that look interesting.

Searching. *I have my résumé and letter ready in plain text, I have my objectives identified, and I am ready to job hunt!*

Choose some specific terms, such as "accounting" and "employment or jobs," and use a search engine or indexer to search for occurrences of those words. Virtual libraries might also be useful here.

> **Internet Tip: Virtual libraries** are collections of links to Internet resources and services arranged by broad topic, similar to the way your library arranges its materials on the shelves.

Establishing Your Internet Attack

Not all parts of the Internet are created equally, or at least they don't carry the same kinds of information. The Internet is really several interlinked databases of information, and each is a little different from the next. As you look around, you'll notice these differences in the types of information and resources you find. How do you decide where to go and what to look at? Consider these two questions while you are planning where to begin and how to move around most effectively.

1. What type of information is usually found here? Is it a formal or informal discussion? Are interests primarily academic, or are there other organizations here? Is it merely job listings or is there other useful information as well?
2. How volatile is the information found here? Is it updated or altered daily, weekly, or monthly? Do postings expire quickly or remain for an extended amount of time?

Mailing lists and some areas of the Usenet tend to be formal in their discussions, whereas other areas of the Usenet are more informal. Gophers tend to be the realm of academe, government, and nonprofit organizations, whereas everyone is on the World Wide Web. Telnet sites are found less frequently, but the community freenets are mostly accessed via Telnet. Usenet newsgroups, mailing lists, and many listings on the World Wide Web change frequently, but Gophers, electronic journals, and Telnet sites tend to change less frequently. As always, there are exceptions, so be sure to look at each site or collection of resources and judge for yourself.

Examining the Internet Network Resources

We've discussed the fact that many parts of the Internet have different characteristics in terms of the type of information usually found and the rate of change. Let's now look at these resources and see what each has to offer the job seeker. We'll also add some comments about the software programs needed to access them.

Usenet Newsgroups

- Find job listings, post résumés, and discuss job hunting. Use groups dedicated to specific topics for networking contacts, industry trends, current information, and job listings.
- Newsgroups can be international, national, local, or organizational in their geographic coverage.
- Information is added daily, even hourly! Groups require frequent monitoring for new information and listings.
- Software: A **newsreader** program like **Tin**.

The Usenet newsgroups are great for current information and for networking contacts in different organizations or other geographic areas. Recruiters and employers are beginning to use the résumés posted on the **misc.jobs.resumes** newsgroup as a database to find prospective employees, so think about placing your résumé here. The ***.jobs** groups (those newsgroups with the word **"jobs"** in their name) are good sources for job listings, but if you step beyond these into the groups that discuss topics in each occupation, field, or discipline, you will find people to get to know and some more specific job listings. To get to know the people on a newsgroup, you must participate in the list discussion by posting and responding to messages if you feel qualified to offer your knowledge or opinion.

Newsgroup Tip: Make sure you know what you are doing before you post so you do not become the victim of those nasty messages called "flames." Think of each newsgroup as a meeting or an office party where you are the new person in the office who must introduce himself. You want to make a good impression your first time out there. Watch a newsgroup for a couple of weeks before you begin posting and get an idea of the culture of each list. Read the **FAQs** for each group, available at **http://www.cis.ohio-state.edu/hypertext/faq/usenet/index.html.**

Mailing Lists

- Occasional job postings, usually well in advance of print announcements. Good networking resource. Information about current topics and interests.
- Lists cover topics similar to those on Usenet newsgroups, but are usually more academic or professional in nature.
- Check your e-mail daily for announcements. Response is not needed immediately, but should not be delayed.
- Software: a **mailer** program like **Pine**, **Elm**, or **Eudora**.

These are not as fast-paced as the newsgroups, and unlike newsgroups which you must remember to read, these are very neatly delivered to your e-mail box. They are a bit more formal in their discussion than the Usenet newsgroups, but they cover many of the same topics. Again, participation is the key. Watch a mailing list for a while to see what the topics of discussion are and what the tone of the list is. Introduce yourself to the other list members and ask questions or offer your advice and opinion if you feel qualified. You can form some great networking contacts in mailing lists if you are a regular participant.

Mailing List Tip: To join a mailing list, send an e-mail message to the listserv, listproc, or majordomo, whichever is the computer operating the distribution of the list. Leave the **subject** blank, and in the body of the mail type "***subscribe listname yourfirstname yourlastname***" as shown here:

To: *listproc@harold.lemon.com*
Subject:
subscribe moneybags Emily Dickinson

> In this instance, Emily Dickinson has joined the mailing list Moneybags at the computer site harold.lemon.com. To send messages to the other readers of this list, she sends her e-mail to moneybags@harold.lemon.com.

Jim Milles at the St. Louis University School of Law has written an excellent guide to using the various mailing list programs. You can get a copy by e-mail or FTP. *These instructions must be typed exactly as you see them with their capital and lower case letters as shown.*

E-mail	FTP
To: Listserv@ubvm.cc.buffalo.edu	ftp ubvm.cc.buffalo.edu
Subject: *leave blank*	cd nettrain
GET MAILSER CMD NETTRAIN F=MAIL	get mailser.cmd

You will also find a copy of this guide on the World Wide Web at **http://lawlib.slu.edu/training/mailser.htm**.

Electronic Journals

- Watch industry trends, keep up with current information, and look for networking contacts. Many carry job ads like their print companions.
- Many titles are free, but others charge a subscription fee.
- Check regularly for new issues.
- Software: a **mailer** program or a **Web browser**.

These were originally academic in focus, but that has changed. Some operate via e-mail, but many are available on Gopher or the Web. Many articles include e-mail addresses for the authors. Use these to contact the authors *very politely* and ask questions about their work and other projects. Even a compliment about an article could open the door to a new contact. If you are examining electronic journals for job listings, remember that a publication's intended audience (academic, corporate, general) will determine the type of job announcements included. Any journal that charges a subscription fee should be willing to send you a free copy for examination. Ask for a sample before buying.

Job Search Tip: If your job search includes an *electronic journal* on a Gopher or Web server, make a note of each new issue in your calendar so you will remember to read it when it is updated.

Telnet Sites

- Good for job listings, but some services might include other information resources or contact information.
- Listings may change daily or weekly, or on a specific day each month.
- Check sites a minimum of once a week or whenever new listings are expected.
- Software: **Telnet**

Telnet is the basic protocol that defines the Internet, namely in the form of the **Telnet Connect Protocol/Internet (TCP/IP) protocol** If you have access to Telnet, you can use it to get to library catalogs, freenets, and public Gopher and Web clients so you can access those networks. These sites can be difficult to locate, but they have some very unique resources. The freenets are great resources for job listings and local information for the regions they serve. Many sites are moving to alternate access through Gopher or the Web, but it is a slow process and may not be everyone's goal. Always read any files that talk about the service to get an idea of its purpose.

Telnet Tip: If you connect to your network over a modem, your modem program probably has the same escape command as Telnet, **control-]** (*control-right bracket*). If that is the case, change your Telnet escape character so you don't get dumped from your modem if you need to get out of Telnet in a hurry.

>telnet

telnet>set escape!

telnet>*escape character!*

telnet>open dice.com

Always note the exit commands. Each site you connect to can have different commands for exiting or moving around the system.

Gopher Servers

- Major resource for academic institutions, professional societies, and the U. S. government. Many freenets here.
- Networking and support, information resources, and job listings are available.
- Software: **Gopher** client or **Web browser**.

This is a great network for job hunters wanting to work in academe, research, or the federal government. Although the growth rate of this network has slowed, it hasn't stopped. Many new servers are being registered both in and out of the United States. Most institutions include their job listings on their servers, so you can target places specifically or use the **geographic listing of Gophers** (see **"All the Gopher Servers in the World"** in the resource list) to locate organizations within a region. Sites should be checked on a regular basis and update schedules noted. This network is a fantastic research resource for information to support your job search and help you with some directions and decisions. Many sites include directories with employee names, job titles, and phone numbers on their gophers.

Gopher Tip: You can connect directly to a Gopher site by adding the address of the host to the Gopher command. This is referred to as "**pointing your Gopher**," and it saves you time in connecting. Selecting an item from the Gopher menu is also referred to as pointing because you are moving the arrow, or pointer, up and down the list.

>**gopher una.hh.lib.umich.edu**

point to (choose) ***inetdirs/***

Clearinghouse for Subject-Oriented Internet Resource Guides

World Wide Web Resources

- Professional societies, academic institutions, and U.S. government agencies. Recruiters and other career-service agencies can be found here.
- Networking contacts, information resources, and job listings are available.
- Information is updated daily on some servers.
- Great network for job hunters in all areas.
- Software: a Web browser such as **Lynx**, **Mosaic**, or **Netscape**.

The Web has taken the lead in Internet resource development, partly due to the participation of so many nonacademic organizations. It is growing faster than any other Internet network at this time, and even the commercial services like CompuServe and Prodigy are including Web access for their users. It's fun, simple to use, and remarkably flexible in how it displays and delivers information. *Remember that this is still only one piece of the Internet.* Don't ignore the other resources and networks available.

> **Job Search Tip:** Bundle your resources and networks so you can use one software program as much as possible. This will save you time and frustration. A **Web browser** such as Mosaic, Netscape, or Lynx can handle Gopher, Web, and most FTP sites, so plan to combine these resources into one search. You might be able to configure it to read news and Telnet also, but check that possibility with your local system help desk.

Questions on Starting Your Search

1. ***I'm just starting out and I'd like to see what is available out there in terms of job listings. Where do I begin?***

   A good way to get a broad overview is to look at the major recruiting services like the **Online Career Center** and the many job guides on the Internet. We've covered these in Chapter 4, but you can also link to these through one guide, **Employment Opportunities and Job Resources on the Internet.** This guide includes over 400 links to job listings and information resources on the Internet which are all useful for the job search. Use it as a starting point for your browsing and searching and to double-check sites that are not responding:

   http://www.wpi.edu/~mfriley/jobguide.html (best address)

   http://www.wpi.edu/Academics/IMS/Library/jobguide/

2. ***I'm looking for work in a specific field. Where do I look for information and job listings in that field?***

   One of the best ways to find employment information in a specific field is to find a good site dedicated to that field. Colleges and universities frequently collect information for their own use in many subjects, and they put it on their public Web and Gopher servers. These sites usually include information on finding employment, research resources, and links to other similar sites. Many professional societies are now on the Internet, and, even if you are not a member, you can use their public information to help with your search. The many **virtual libraries** on the Internet can also be used in this way, and we've included several in the list of resources on page 34.

3. ***I'm going to be moving and I'd like to begin my job search now. Is there any way I can do it?***

   Absolutely! Both the **Web** and **Gopher** have lists of registered servers which are arranged by geographic location. Choose where you want to be and begin examining the servers in that area for information and opportunities. The **Freenets** are also a great way to begin your search, and there are several ways to locate these through the **virtual libraries** and the **HYTELNET** program. Many of the ***.jobs newsgroups** on the **Usenet** are also specific to a geographic region, so you can read newsgroups for the area you are moving to and begin contacting employers now.

4. ***I really want to work for XYZ company. How can I find information about them and see if they have any positions available?***

   Use a search engine like the **WWW Worm** or the **WebCrawler** to search a company's name as a keyword. Check the **Open Market Commercial Sites Index** to see if it is included in that listing. If you know where the company is located, you can use the **Master List of WWW Servers** to find their Web server. Also check the **virtual libraries** for links to the company under a variety of headings, such as "business" or "commerce." Once you connect to their site, look for "Personnel" or "Human Resources." Many organizations now put their job listings on their front page, so you shouldn't have to look very far.

The General Internet Job Search Strategy

In working with job seekers I have found the following three-step process for conducting your online job search to be an effective approach to managing your online time and structuring your search. In fact, in speaking with a man I consider one of the pioneers of online career services, I was both surprised and pleased to hear him identify the same three steps! Use these steps as you identify your target sites and resources, and keep using them while you are conducting your job search.

1. **Visit the large recruiting and job-listing databases first.** The number of positions, the variety of occupations and fields, and the keyword-searchable indexes make it very easy for you to search these databases fast and effectively.
2. **Move on to the smaller, more exclusive recruiting and job-listing services.** Identify those that have listings for your occupation and discipline, and bookmark or hotlist them.
3. **Use the indexers and search engines to begin locating resources specific to your occupation and field.** Use these sites to locate specific organizations and companies to contact and to look for even smaller, more exclusive collections of job listings. Don't forget about mailing lists and Usenet newsgroups either.

Internet Tip: Your Web browser has a feature called either a *bookmark* or a *hotlist* that permits you to save a customized list of sites in a menu. This lets you connect to them quickly when you want to look at them again. Check the pull-down menus in your graphical browser to see where this is. In Lynx, use the "A" command to add the item to your bookmark list.

Resources for Finding Internet Information and Listings

This list includes starting points for locating Internet information and is divided into three categories: **online guides and resource lists**, **virtual libraries**, and **indexers and search engines**. Search these resources not just for job listings or employment information, but also for information about your field or discipline. This may present more possibilities for networking or researching your career choices. Search the names of companies and other organizations in the search engines, or by looking for links within subject guides and virtual libraries.

A note about the resources addresses: Internet addresses for all servers and resources are given in the form of a **uniform resource locator** (**URL**). The URL consists of two pieces of information—how to connect and the address to connect to—separated by a colon and two slash marks. Additional information on the directory and file name might be included, and these are separated from each other by slash marks:

how to connect://where to connect/directory path to follow/what to get

http://www.wpi.edu/~mfriley/jobguide.html

gopher://una.hh.lib.umich.edu/inetdirs/

> **Internet Tip:** If you have trouble connecting to a site, try chopping the URL back one slash mark. The file or directory you are seeking may have moved, and by backing up one level at a time you may be able to find the new location.

Online Guides and Resource Lists

All of the Gopher Servers in the World (The Mother Gopher)

gopher://gopher.micro.umn.edu:70

select Other Gopher and Information Servers

"The **Mother Gopher**" is the central registry for the Gopher network. This primarily comprises lists of servers arranged geographically, making it easy to target those in a particular location. This list can be displayed in its entirety by selecting "All of the Gophers in the World," but it is recommended that you use the other geographic listings instead. Use the **Veronica** indexer (listed on page 36) to search this network.

Master WWW Server List

http://www.w3.org/hypertext/DataSources/WWW/Servers.html

The central registry of Web servers arranged geographically. Formerly housed at CERN in Switzerland, these files have been transferred to the World Wide Web Organization (W3O). It's similar in function to *The Mother Gopher* list. I still think of this as the center of the Web, if such a place can be identified.

Clearinghouse for Subject-Oriented Internet Resource Guides (The Clearinghouse)

http://www.lib.umich.edu/chhome.html

gopher://una.hh.lib.umich.edu/11/inetdirs/

A great starting place to search for all types of Internet-accessible information. An index to all guides is available and can be searched using keywords. The "**http**" address will take you to both the text Gopher guides and the hypertext Web guides, whereas the **Gopher** address will only give you access to the text guides. Some of the guides in the clearinghouse cover online job hunting, government resources, business and economic information, and nonprofit organizations on the Internet.

The Scholarly Societies Project, University of Waterloo Library

http://www.lib.uwaterloo.ca/society/overview.html

This site contains links to all of the scholarly and professional academic societies with servers on the Internet. Many organizations include job listings and career-related information for their members, so this is a good place to look for job opportunities and information, especially those in academe or those requiring advanced degrees. Organizations also include their journals and newsletters in electronic form, as well as links to related information resources on the Internet.

Open Market's Commercial Sites Index

http://www.directory.net/

This is a searchable index of commercial services, products, and information on the Internet. You can also browse the alphabetical list of all entries, but that is not recommended unless you are absolutely desperate. This is one of the best ways to target companies on the Internet who might be looking for someone like you.

Net-Happenings Archive

http://www.mid.net:80/NET/

This mailing list archive monitors several lists announcing new Internet resources. These servers are the principle information resources for this service, which is a recommended place to search for all types of new Internet resources.

Netlink

http://netlink.wlu.edu:1020

gopher://netlink.wlu.edu:1020

The Netlink server contains links to high-level sources on the Internet, primarily at the root or home-page site levels. You can search this list by selecting the main search option or by choosing one of the predefined menus: Subject, Type (Gopher, Telnet, and so on), Geographic, or Domain.

List of All Active Newsgroups

ftp://ftp.uu.net

login: anonymous, **password**: **your e-mail address**
cd usenet/news.answers/active-newsgroups
get the files part1.Z *and* part2.Z

List of All Usenet Newsgroups

ftp://ftp.uu.net

login: *anonymous*, **password:** *your e-mail address*
cd networking/news/config
get newsgroups.Z

These files try to keep up with the changes and specifications of all Usenet newsgroups. The *List of All Newsgroups* includes many of the local and organization hierarchies available on Usenet. *Warning:* These files are enormous! They are also compressed using the Unix or GNU compression programs. You'll need to find out how to uncompress them and what software can do this for you.

> **Internet Tip: FTP** is the Internet method of copying a file from a remote site to your local computer. **Anonymous FTP** means that you use "anonymous" as the login or user name when you connect to a site and then give your full e-mail address as your password. To use FTP, type "*ftp*" and the address of the computer you want to connect to at your network prompt. Once connected, you "*change directory*" to the one you want, "*get*" the file, and *quit*.

>ftp ftp.csd.uwm.edu

username: anonymous

Guest login ok; give userid as password: you@your.email.address

ftp>cd pub

ftp>get inet.services.txt

ftp>quit

Publicly Accessible Mailing Lists (PAML)

http://www.neosoft.com/internet/paml/

A searchable list of mailing lists currently maintained by Stephanie da Silva. It is similar to the **SRI List of Lists** (next listing), but features a keyword search to locate listings easily.

SRI List of Lists

ftp sri.com

login: anonymous, **password:** your e-mail address
cd netinfo
get interest-groups.txt

This site, a huge list of Internet mailing lists, gets busy, so you may want to try it at off-peak hours. The file is around 1 MB, so be prepared when you download it.

Directory of Academic Discussion Lists (Kovacs List)

http://www.mid.net/KOVACS/

Compiled and edited by Diane Kovacs, this is the primary resource for finding academic mailing lists on the Internet. This information is also included in the *Directory of Electronic Journals, Newsletters, and Academic Discussion Lists.*

Indiana University Mailing List Archive

http://scwww.ucs.indiana.edu/mlarchive/

This is another good list of Internet mailing lists and is searchable by keywords.

Directory of Electronic Journals, Newsletters, and Academic Discussion Lists

gopher://arl.cni.org (Association of Research Libraries)
select Scholarly Communications
select Directory of Electronic Journals...

To find a list of available electronic mailing lists, journals, and newsletters, you can search this directory edited by Diane Kovacs and others. A print copy may be obtained from the Association of Research Libraries in Washington, DC.

NewJour—The Archive of New Electronic Journal Announcements

http://govt.ucsd.edu.newjour

This is the archive for the NewJour mailing list and contains all announcements of new electronic journals for the past few years. Used in conjunction with the *Directory of Electronic Journals*, you can find electronic journals in almost any field.

Internet Tip: Telnet Access to the Web. If you have Telnet capability but no access to the Web, you can **telnet** to a public Web server using the following addresses:

- telnet.w3.org **login:** www
- sunsite.unc.edu **login:** lynx

Virtual Libraries

The Galaxy at TradeWave

http://galaxy.einet.net/galaxy.html

Highly recommended as a beginning point when searching for information on the World Wide Web. The Galaxy has both a virtual library and a search engine, and maintains links to other similar sites. Search for information on a particular topic, or try to identify an organization by searching for its name.

Library of Congress

http://lcweb.loc.gov/

gopher://marvel.loc.gov/

Although not a "virtual library" in the strictest sense, the Library of Congress provides access to all other federal agencies on the Internet through its Gopher and Web servers, and additional guides and pointers to more information resources throughout the Internet. It also hosts the THOMAS server, which carries information on legislation from the 103rd and 104th Congresses.

RiceInfo

http://riceinfo.rice.edu/RiceInfo/Subject.html

gopher://riceinfo.rice.edu:70 (RiceInfo, Rice University CWIS) *select* Information by Subject

A great site of information links arranged by subject, this library is highly recommended for finding Gopher information if Veronica is not accessible. It's very nicely done.

Virtual Library (W3O)

http://www.w3.org/hypertext/DataSources/bySubject/Overview.html

Formerly CERN's library of links, this list is now maintained by the World Wide Web Organization. Topics are arranged by broad categories and contain some interesting information.

Whole Internet Catalogue

http://gnn.com/wic/wics/index.html

This is the resource list from *The Whole Internet User's Guide* by Ed Krol. It is updated on a regular basis. Krol's book was probably the first Internet "bible."

Yahoo

http://www.yahoo.com/

A list of links arranged by subject with a wonderful search index over it all, Yahoo is one of the (if not *the*) largest sites for searching out information on the Internet. It's an absolutely fantastic starting point for information on the Web. Yahoo has the best search engine available. A keyword search on "Employment" turned up hundreds of sites, with more added on a regular basis. Unfortunately, since everyone knows how good it is, it frequently gets very busy.

Indexers and Search Engines

HYTELNET

http://galaxy.einet.net/hytelnet/HYTELNET.html
http://library.usask.ca/hytelnet/
gopher://marvel.loc.gov/ (Library of Congress)
select Internet Resources
select HYTELNET

Originally a program designed to track library catalogs available through Telnet, this is now a major resource for locating and connecting to sites accessible via Telnet. The Web version includes a keyword search mechanism. Peter Scott created and maintains this program. You can find job listings and links to regional information and some organizations using this program. Try a keyword search on "Employment."

Veronica

gopher://gopher.scs.unr.edu:70 (University of Nevada, Reno)
select Search ALL of Gopherspace...

This is the main index to Gopher information. It can be problematic to use due to its size, but it does have great value. You can search it using keywords in various combinations to find and connect to information at various Gopher sites. Read the "How to Compose Veronica Queries" file before beginning your search.

Jughead

gopher://marvel.loc.gov (Library of Congress)
select Internet Resources
select Veronica and Jughead

Jughead is a smaller, more customized index to Gopher. The indexing is not as extensive as in Veronica, so the search results are smaller and easier to manage.

WebCrawler

http://webcrawler.com

A great search index for information on the World Wide Web, WebCrawler lets you search by keywords, such as a field you are interested in or the name of a company or organization you are seeking.

WWW Worm

http://www.cs.colorado.edu/WWWW/

This is a highly recommended and easy-to-use search program for finding information on the Web. You search by selecting various fields or parts of a page of information. Information on organizations is easy to locate using the "Document Title" and "URL Address" features.

Internet Tip: Accessing the Internet by E-Mail. If you only have e-mail access to the Internet, you can still get Web pages and everything else. Send the following message to the address indicated to get a copy of *Accessing the Internet by E-Mail* by Bob Rankin (bobrankin@delphi.com):

To: LISTSERV@ubvm.cc.buffalo.edu (for US/Canada/etc.)

Leave Subject blank, and enter only this line in the body of the note:

GET INTERNET BY E-MAIL NETTRAIN F = MAIL

To: MAILBASE@mailbase.ac.uk (for UK/Europe/etc.)

Leave Subject blank, and enter only this line in the body of the note:

send lis-iis e-access-inet.txt

Bob is working on a print version of this, so keep watching the bookstores and your public library for copies!

Additional Reading about the Online Job Search

These books can provide more information on electronic job searching or may present an angle or some information we did not include here. Check your library for availability.

- **Dixon, Pam, and Sylvia Tiersten.** *Be Your Own Headhunter Online*. New York: Random House, 1995.
- **Glossbrenner, Alfred and Emily.** *Finding a Job on the Internet*. New York: McGraw-Hill, 1995.
- **Gonyea, James C.** *The On-Line Job Search Companion*. New York: McGraw-Hill, 1995.
- **Jandt, Fred E., and Mary B. Nemnich.** *Using the Internet in Your Job Search*. Indianapolis, IN: JIST, 1995.
- **Kennedy, Joyce Lain.** *Electronic Job Search Revolution*. New York: Wiley, 1994.
- ———. *Electronic Résumé Revolution*. New York: Wiley, 1994.
- ———. *Hook up, Get Hired!* New York: Wiley, 1995.
- **Snell, Alice.** *The Job Seeker's Guide to On-Line Resources, 2nd ed*. Fitzwilliam, NH: Kennedy Publications, 1995.

CHAPTER 4

Great Job Listing Sites

This chapter lists the sites and services on the Internet known for their collected job listings. They cover multiple fields and disciplines, providing leads for almost every job you can think of. What has been included here?

1. **Usenet newsgroups.** These deal primarily with the **misc.jobs.*** collection of newsgroups. Most other newsgroups are included with the local (**Chapter 10**) or international listings (**Chapter 12**).
2. **Online recruiting services.** These are recruiters and other organizations posting job announcements on the Internet. They are primarily U.S. recruiters, but most of these sites carry listings for both U.S. and international jobs. Sites recruiting specifically for academe can be found in **Chapter 7**, and sites recruiting internationally have been included in **Chapter 12**.
3. **Online guides to the job hunt.** Guides give you tips and pointers along with their lists of resources. Most, but not all, of them cover Internet resources exclusively. This list includes the online addresses for Harry's Job Search BBS & Internet Hot List (**see Appendix B**).
4. **Links to more online job resources.** You may find duplications, you may find yourself back where you began, but you may also find things others haven't yet added. These do not necessarily guide you in your search or provide information about a site before you connect to it.

> **Job Search Tip:** When an employer pulls your résumé off the Net and invites you for an interview, you place yourself at a disadvantage if you fail to ask him or her to send information about the company. Experiences are surfacing about candidates who enter Net-generated interviews without a clue as to what the company does or makes or where it is headed. Remember the old "research first" rule, only updated for technology.
> **Joyce Lain Kennedy**, *syndicated careers columnist; author of Hook Up, Get Hired!*

Usenet Newsgroups

*These newsgroups are specifically for job posting unless otherwise indicated in their descriptions. Please do not post résumés or begin discussions in newsgroups that are not specifically set up for these things. See the note on **"flaming"** in* **Chapter 3**.

biz.jobs.offered

Commercial postings of jobs available all over.

misc.jobs.offered

General positions available, although jobs in technology (computing and software) tend to dominate this group. This group sometimes sees as many as 500 new listings a day, so read it frequently if you want to include it in your search.

misc.jobs.offered.entry

Entry-level positions available; one to two years experience sometimes preferred.

misc.jobs.contract

Contract positions; usually short term and with minimal benefits. This could be a good way to find temporary employment when you are between jobs.

misc.jobs.resumes

The place to post your résumé in ASCII or text format only. Recruiters and employers scan this newsgroup regularly looking for potential employees. Read it for ideas on your own résumé. *Please do not post jobs here.*

misc.jobs.wanted

People looking for jobs. You can post your "dream job" and see if anyone has something like it to offer you.

Online Recruiting Services

These services recruit through job listings primarily in, but not necessarily limited to, the United States. Some of these services may carry academic positions, but their general feel is nonacademic.

America's Job Bank

http://www.ajb.dni.us/

telnet ajb.dni.us

A joint effort of the hundreds of offices of the State Employment Service. Access is available via the Web or Telnet, but the Web access is better. You can search this database in a variety of ways—keywords, job code from your state employment office, and even military occupation codes. These are jobs that the offices are unsuccessful in filling locally, so listings in individual state employment offices and on the ALEX system usually are not duplicated here.

Online Career Center

http://www.occ.com/

gopher://occ.com

One of the first Internet recruiting services, and probably the largest. This service includes a database of job listings that can be searched by geographic regions or keywords and a free résumé bank. It also has a number of great information resources for the job hunter, including links to information on internships and several colleges and universities. Employer information and guides to the job search make this a full-service resource for job seekers.

E-Span, The Interactive Employment Network

http://www.espan.com/

One of the largest recruiters on the Internet. E-Span provides a searchable database of job openings, as well as a wide variety of resources for the job seeker. To search its extensive database of job listings, choose a keyword and then select a category from the many broad fields indicated. Like other services of this type, it includes a tremendous amount of great information for the job search. Questions about this service can be addressed to info@espan3.espan.com.

CareerMosaic

http:///www.careermosaic.com/cm/

This online recruiting service is run by Bernard Hodes, Inc. Job listings can be searched by keyword, or you can choose a listed company and view their available positions. Great information about each company is included. There is a tremendous amount of fantastic job-hunting information here, along with a searchable archive of several Usenet jobs newsgroups. Résumés are accepted for inclusion in the résumé bank at no charge.

The Monster Board

http://www.monster.com/

The Monster Board is operated by ADION Information Services, a division of ADION, Inc., a large recruitment advertising agency in New England. It offers an overview of employers and several interfaces for job hunting. You can search by company name, location, discipline, industry, job title, or combinations of these. The employer overview gives some background information about the company selected, its products and services, and employee benefits. The service also has a tremendous database of information for the job seeker and the employer. You can register your résumé with The Monster Board or use its online application to apply for positions listed here. For more information, call (800) MONSTER.

Career Magazine

http://www.careermag.com/careermag/

This online career information magazine includes job listings, employer profiles, a searchable résumé bank, a directory of recruiters, and news and articles related to today's job hunt. *Career Magazine* also scans and archives job announcements from several Usenet newsgroups to permit easy searching and access. The Jobnet Forum allows you to discuss your job search and ask questions.

Help Wanted USA

http://www.webcom.com/~career/hwusa.html

The original service from Gonyea and Associates, Inc., which is found all over the information superhighway. James Gonyea should be credited with the establishment of career and employment resources in the online environment. Help Wanted's listings are found on the Online Career Center and America Online, but they are adding new services with several recruiting centers located throughout the United States.

Contract Employment Weekly, Jobs Online

http://www.ceweekly.wa.com/

gopher://gopher.ceweekly.wa.com

This service, originally a newspaper, specializes in listings for contract employees, usually short term. It has two sets of job listings online, one for subscribers and one for nonsubscribers. Even with that restriction, there is a lot of information here and several listings. If you have never worked on contract before, you should read the file on contract work. The Web site is better than the Gopher.

The Internet Professional Association, including the Recruiters OnLine Network

http://www.ipa.com/ipa/

A virtual organization and association supporting recruiters and recruiting on the Internet. This site offers a database of users, resources for recruiters as well as current job searchers, and an area for individuals to post résumés for perusal by members of this service. Plans are underway for space where recruiters can post current searches. This site also includes tips on job hunting and articles on using recruiters in the job search.

JobWeb

http://www.jobweb.com/

The JobWeb trademark is owned by the National Association of Colleges and Employers (NACE) in Bethlehem, P.A. This is a well-designed site featuring an electronic gateway to career planning and employment information; job-search articles and tips; job listings; and company information for college students, recent graduates, alumni, and career service professionals. NACE was formerly known as the College Placement Council. For more information, call (800) 544-5272.

BAMTA, Bay Area Multiple Technology Alliance

http://mlds-www.arc.nasa.gov/form/BAMTA/

The Bay Area Multimedia Technology Alliance (BAMTA) job bank is a part of the Web Form technology project. BAMTA provides this Web space for posting job openings. Job hunters from anywhere can view the listed positions or post their "dream job" for others to see. Recruiters and employers can list their open positions in a variety of fields for easy searching by job hunters. All of this is free of charge and forms are provided online for users. Contact **chu@mlds-www.arc.nasa.gov** with any questions.

Employment Edge

http: //www.employmentedge.com/employment.edge/

Employment Edge specializes in professional career placement throughout the United States. Confidentiality is assured and there is never a fee of any kind to candidates. Applications and résumés for positions listed here are accepted via fax or e-mail. At last check, it had several listings for accounting and legal work along with several areas of management and technology.

Career Connections' H.E.A.R.T.

http://www.career.com

telnet career.com

telnet college.career.com (*entry-level listings*)

login with your first and last name and select a password

(CAREER CONNECTIONS) H.E.A.R.T., "Human Resources Electronic Advertising & Recruiting Tool," is a menu-driven system with presentations of career opportunities. There is no charge to the job seeker. When you first connect, you will be asked to register and select a password so a private e-mail and profile account can be created for you. You can apply for jobs through this system, but to do so you must create an online "profile," so have a copy of your résumé at hand. Web access still requires Telnet to reach the job database. Questions or problems connecting? Call **(415) 903-5800** or send e-mail to **postmaster@career.com.**

JobBank USA

http://www.jobbankusa.com/

Absolutely fantastic resource for job searching! The Job Bank accepts résumés in ASCII format via e-mail for distribution at no charge for six months. There is a fee to input your résumé if you cannot e-mail it. The services included are diverse and interesting. Send e-mail to exchange@mindspring.com.

GetAJob!!!

http://www.teleport.com/~pcllgn/gaj.html

Links to various job-related sites, employers, and open-position listings. The best parts of this service are "**JobsJobsJobs**," which has links to corporate recruiting pages; "**Companies**", which links to companies without recruiting pages but with contact information; and "**Services**," which links to other Internet services and databases for your job search.

Help Wanted.Com, YSS Inc.

http://www.helpwanted.com/

This company specializes in career opportunity development and support, and it offers recruiting services in the university arena, data management, market research, and management. Job listings are searchable by keyword, or you can examine the various companies included and see all of their available positions. This is a service of YSS, Inc. (Your Software Solutions) in Marlborough, MA.

Career Web

http://www.cweb.com/

Owned by Landmark Communications, this multipurpose site has job listings, an extensive career library, information on employers, and a career fitness test you can take to see how you are doing and where you are going. Point Survey has rated it among the top ten sites on The Net. Further development is under way with new listings and services.

IntelliMatch

http://www.intellimatch.com/

IntelliMatch is an online database service that allows its clients to search directly for the individuals they are looking for by matching their requirements to registered skills. The matching is done by the employers from their computers, so you interact directly with the hiring managers of the various organizations. IntelliMatch has developed an interesting form for this process, which you will need to fill out in order to be included in this database. Also included is a fantastic area called The Job Center with listings, articles about the job search, and links to more Internet resources.

The Internet Job Locator

http://mtc.globesat.com/jobs/

You will need a forms-capable browser to use this site. Your search can be done by keyword or by choosing a state, city, and job category. Information on jobs includes contact information for applications. Questions can be sent to mtc@gslink.net.

JobCenter

http://www.jobcenter.com/

JobCenter offers an interesting service. Post your résumé here and let the service do the searching for you. Each day you'll receive new relevant ads right in your e-mail box. You can also perform online searches with JobCenter. It gives you control of the distribution of your résumé. You can examine job ads and résumés online, complete with hypertext links, without having to subscribe to the service. However, you will not be able to add your résumé or job listing without subscribing, nor will you be notified automatically of new jobs or résumés. Regular mail can be sent to JobCenter, 1541 East Lake Road, Skaneateles, NY 13152; phone: (800) JOBCENTER (562-2368); e-mail address: info@jobcenter.com. If you are outside the United States call (315) 673-0122.

National Association of Personnel Services: Member Resource Center

http://naps.resourcecenter.com/

NAPS (Temporary/Permanent Placement Services Firms Association) represents about 1,000 personnel service firms in government affairs, public relations, education, certification, and ethical standards. Member firms adhere to industry standards and practices. The site is constructing a directory of member firms which could be useful to the job seeker trying to identify which temporary placement firms to contact. Send e-mail to naps@iag.com.

JobTrak

http://www.jobtrak.com

A service that permits the students and alumni of member institutions to view job listings online at no cost. Your college or university must be a member for you to gain access to the job listings, but the many information resources and the list of employers can be viewed by all. If your institution is listed as a member, contact the career office for the password. If your institution is not included, the list of employers can give you some leads for possible employment.

Career Web, The Huntington Group

http://www.sgx.com/cw/

This site is maintained by The Huntington Group, a professional search firm for the high-tech industry. Résumés are accepted via e-mail or can be submitted online using a forms-capable browser. Even though the recruiting company is a high-tech specialist, jobs in many other areas are included here, along with other resources for an Internet job search.

NationJob

http://www.nationjob.com

NationJob is an online job-search database sponsored by NationJob, a privately held corporation in Ankeny, IA. This database contains listings for thousands of jobs open around the United States (primarily in the Midwest), and you may specify conditions that will show you only the jobs you may be interested in. You can view jobs by category, search for companies that meet your criteria, or examine companies with jobs listed. Jobs are updated weekly. If you cannot use the forms, the list of organizations (and there are a lot) have their open job listings attached. Positions listed have good information but no dates. Contact NationJob via e-mail at NationJ@worf.infonet.net, or by phone at (800) 292-7731.

College Grad Job Hunter

http://www.collegegrad.com/

Quantum Leap Publishing maintains this site which provides links to career resources, job sites, and companies. As its name implies, it is geared to the college graduate. Send e-mail to insider@execpc.com.

NetJobs

http://www.netjobs.com: 8000/index.html

The NetJobs server provides a database of current job openings arranged by category, company/organization, location, or those posted in the last ten days. Each listing includes the contact information for application. For a fee, you can add your résumé to the online database.

Saludos Web Site

http://www.hooked.net/saludos/

This Web site, dedicated exclusively to promoting Hispanic careers and education, is supported by *Saludos Hispanos* magazine. Information includes job listings and other good career information; an "Education Center" with announcements of internships, mentoring programs, and scholarship opportunities; the "Résumé Pool" where Hispanic job seekers can post their résumés; recent articles from *Saludos Hispanos*; and links to additional Internet resources of interest to the Hispanic community. Comments and questions can be sent to **erikac@saludos.com.**

J. Robert Scott

http://j-robert-scott.com/

Founded in 1986, J. Robert Scott is a retainer-based executive search firm specializing in the recruitment of senior-level professionals and managers across a broad range of industries, including financial services, telecommunications, software, retail, biotechnology, and health care. The jobs listed have good descriptions and include job titles, but organizational information is confidential. You can see a list of some past clients in the page of company information. The firm is headquartered in Boston, but the practice is international in scope. For more information, contact J. Robert Scott, 27 State Street, Boston, MA 02109; phone: (617) 720-2770; fax (617) 723-1282; e-mail: info@j-robert-scott.com. *See Appendix A for more information on executive searches.*

SEACnet: Southeastern-Atlantic Coast Career Network

http: //www.virginia.edu/~seacnet/

The career planning offices of the 21 universities making up the Southeastern-Atlantic Coast Career Network have joined together to create a full-fledged recruiting network on the Web. Employers can browse the almost 300 majors to see which schools offer which programs and request résumés from the résumé databases (approximately 400,000 students). A videoconferencing network ties the schools together, so that potential employers can visit any school in the consortium and interview students via videoconference at any of the other 20 during the visit. The 21 schools are: Alabama, Arkansas, Auburn, Clemson, Duke, Florida, Florida State, Georgia, Georgia Tech, Kentucky, Louisiana State, Maryland, Mississippi, Mississippi State, North Carolina, North Carolina State, South Carolina, Tennessee, Vanderbilt, Virginia, and Wake Forest. For more information, contact the career center at any participating university.

Wide World Web Employment Office

http://www.harbornet.com/biz/office/annex.html

This site, sponsored by The Office Annex, is set up to be a great starting point for an Internet job search. Jobs posted here are arranged by major occupation, and additional links to general resources and resources for each occupation area are included. Résumés can be posted for a small fee, and the cost of listing a job here is very low.

The EPages: Jobs Offered Index

http://ep.com/jb.html

EPage is difficult to categorize. Companies as well as job candidates can advertise positions to be filled or positions sought with no charge. Candidates can scan positions by category; the postings give different amounts of information about the jobs listed. Contact via e-mail at epage@ep.com.

Online Guides to the Job Hunt

These are Internet guides for your online job search. They not only gather together online information and resources for you, but they provide evaluations and guidance for your online search.

Employment Opportunities and Job Resources on the Internet

Margaret F. Riley, Internet job-search consultant

http://www.wpi.edu/~mfriley/jobguide.html

http: //www.wpi.edu/Academics/IMS/Library/jobguide/

This guide includes hundreds of links to Internet information resources divided into major fields for your job search. Additionally, the *Riley Guide* includes information on how to use the Internet, incorporating the Internet into your job search, and research resources for your job search. Questions or comments can be sent to **mfriley@wpi.edu**.

Job Search and Employment Opportunities: Best Bets from the Net

Phil Ray and Brad Taylor, University of Michigan

http://asa.ugl.lib.umich.edu/chdocs/employment/

gopher://una.hh.lib.umich.edu/00/inetdirsstacks/employment%3araytay

The guide has selected the best places to begin searching for jobs in various disciplines. It includes easy instructions on using the Internet and links to other resources for more information on both the Internet and Internet job searching.

The Catapult, Career Service Professionals Homepage

The National Association of Colleges and Employers (NACE)

http://www.jobweb.org/CATAPULT/catapult.html

The Catapult is a springboard to the frequently visited sites on Career Service Professionals and contains more than 200 links to career and employment resources found on the Web, with notes about available résumé banks and extensive entry-level positions.

The Entry Level Job Seeker Assistant
Joseph E. Schmalhofer III, University of Tennessee

http://work1.utsi.edu:8000/~jschmalh/jobhome.html

http://galaxy.einet.net/galaxy/Community/Workplace.html

Featured in the June 1995 issue of *NetGuide* as a good source of information on finding an entry-level position through the Internet, this site includes links to online recruiters and organizations who are willing to hire entry-level employees. There is also a place where your HTML résumé can be linked according to your major field or specialty. There are some format specifications for linking your résumé, so please read these before you contact the site administrator. These pages are mirrored on the **Tradewave Galaxy at http: //galaxy.einet.net**, but the original is the more up-to-date site. Questions and comments can be sent to **jschmalh@sparc2000.utsi.edu.**

> **Internet Tip: HTML** is the *HyperText Mark-up Language*, the coding used to create the documents you see on the World Wide Web. It tells the Web browser how to display the document (size of type, placement on the screen, and so on) and lets you create the **hyperlinks** that take you from document to document.

Harry's Job Search BBS Hot List
Harold Lemon, hlemon@netcom.com

http://www.wpi.edu/Academics/IMS/Library/jobguide/harry.html

http://rescomp.stanford.edu/jobs-bbs.html

This list includes bulletin boards (BBS) accessible via modem. The list was started while Harry was job hunting himself, and he found these sites to be very useful, so he is sharing them with others. Each entry gives the name of a BBS, the phone number, modem settings, types of positions listed, and whether or not fees are charged to access these services. This guide is arranged by state. Most of the listings are free services, and Harry checks them all before he adds them to the list and again when he updates it. A copy of this guide is included in Appendix B of this book.

JobHunt: A Meta-list of On-Line Job-Search Resources and Services
Dane Spearing, Assistant Director of Residential Computing, Stanford University

http://rescomp.stanford.edu/jobs.html

A great resource and one of the original Web guides to the Internet job search. Dare Spearing notes which sites are particularly good and includes comments about the resources included in his guide.

Links to More Online Job Listings

These sites have collected extensive lists of links to job resources on the Internet. They do not necessarily provide information about the resources or the online job search, but you may find leads and services not listed in the guides from the previous section. I have listed these in reverse alphabetical order so my favorite site can be first.

Yahoo's Listings of Employment Information

http://www.yahoo.com/Business/Employment

Absolutely fantastic service arranged by broad categories that subdivide. It is very easy to navigate, and it has a search engine you can use to find information within the server. While you are there, check out The Yahoo Homepage at **http://www.yahoo.com/.**

University of Colorado, Boulder

gopher://gopher.Colorado.EDU/
select Other Gophers by Subject
select Employment Opportunities and Résumé Postings

This service is an excellent resource for information on Gopher arranged by subject. The links to employment opportunities include several U.S. colleges and universities along with other major resources included in this book.

Starting Point: Professional

http://www.stpt.com/profe.html

Starting Point is sponsored by Superhighway Consulting, a turnkey Internet provider, and provides links to other job resources rather than listing its own. These include the CareerWeb, the *Chicago Tribune* Career Finder, Career Resource Home Page, and dozens of other helpful sites.

SenseMedia's GetAJob

http://sensemedia.net/getajob/

SenseMedia has put together a great collection of links to Internet job information, including links to jobs for people who are fluent in Japanese and Chinese. This is coded in HTML 3.0 tables, so your browser may not display the links as nicely as they have been laid out.

RPI Career Resources

http://www.rpi.edu/dept/cdc/

The Career Development Center at Rensselaer Polytechnic Institute (RPI) has put together an impressive collection of links to U.S. and international resources. The resources include many links to subject-specific employment listings.

RiceInfo

http://riceinfo.rice.edu/RiceInfo/Subject.html

gopher.//riceinfo.rice.edu/11/Subject/Jobs

RiceInfo from Rice University in Texas is one of the better collections of subject-based Internet information, paying attention to the Gopher network and its resources.

Purdue University SSINFO Gopher

gopher://oasis.cc.purdue.edu: 2525/11/employ-info

Student services information from Purdue is available here.

JobNet

http://www.westga.edu/~coop/

A project of the West Georgia College Career Services, this site includes files to help you write résumés and interview well, and it has extensive links to job resources.

Jobs and Employment

gopher://academic.cc.colorado.edu/11%5b_library._data.jobs%5d

This site at Colorado College (Colorado Springs, CO) contains links to over 100 career, job, and employment sources (college, university, and commercial) in many fields. It also provides foundation and grant information.

Jobs and Career Information

gopher://main.morris.org/11gopher_root%3a%5b_jobs%5d

The Morris Automated Information Network maintains this collection of links to 50 university job and career sites. It includes college and research libraries, university, state government, and federal government job listings. Send questions via e-mail to weinstein@main.morris.org.

Inter-Links Employment Resources

http://www.nova.edu/Inter-Links/employment.html

This is a service of Nova Southeastern University in Florida.

Career Center (from the Internet Professional)

http://www.netline.com/Career/career.html

Netline's Career Center provides WWW links to about a dozen great job-listing sites, including Career Mosaic, H.E.A.R.T., The Monster Board, and the California Career and Employment Center. Contact the center via e-mail at webmaster@netline.com.

CHAPTER 5

Jobs in Business and Related Fields

The resources covered in this chapter provide or point to career information and job postings in business, accounting, human resources, and related fields. If you are skipping around in this book, the job-listing sites in **Chapter 4** are another good place to start your search.

We have *not* included names of specific companies or organizations that are recruiting in these fields, although many of the links listed will take you to those companies. Use the resources given in **Chapter 3** to look for prospective employers on your own. For example, if you are interested in working for a medical firm, use search terms or follow links that relate to the medical field. You can use the **Master List of WWW Servers** to identify organizations or employers of interest. The **Mother Gopher** will not be as much help for commercial organizations, but it can reveal a number of business and related positions in colleges and universities. Keep in mind that even high-tech companies cannot do business without a team of accountants, sales representatives, and managers to help them run efficiently. The opportunities are endless, and this list is just the beginning!

Job Search Tip: Set up your bookmarks with a section for keyword searches. Most job-hunt URLs require you to negotiate several levels before getting to the search page. Having these bookmarked in a readily accessible list means that you can go directly to each search page, put in your keywords, and quickly search the database. If you have a graphical browser, set it for the number of days you want to elapse between each search—three, five, seven, or more. You can then tell by the color of each link when you should search the database again. **Fred Nagel**, *Manager Career Services, ETI / The Career Center, Poughkeepsie, New York.*

Great Starting Points

Business Job Finder

http://www.cob.ohio-state.edu/dept/fin/osujobs.htm

Maintained by Tim Opler, a member of the faculty at Ohio State University, Job Finder is a fantastic collection of links to job listings, information, and recruiting resources for the business or finance specialist, or for someone considering work in these fields.

MIT Sloan School of Management

http: //web.mit.edu/sloan/www

MIT's Sloan School manages this informative site for its students. Included in the publicly accessible resources are a list of employers who have hired Sloan students and/or graduates in the past two years with links to their organizational home pages and a guide to online resources for your job search, including several informational links you can use to find leads.

Accounting and Finance*

AAFA—The American Association Of Finance and Accounting

http://www.marketlink.com:80/aafa/

AAFA has recruiting specialists in accounting and finance. They recruit in 35 states and five international locations. Contact mrklnk@marketlink.com for more information.

RJ Pascale & Company

http://www.ct-jobs.com/pascale/

RJ Pascale & Company is a professional search-and-recruiting firm located in southwestern Connecticut. The firm specializes in placement and staff fulfillment for accounting and EDP professionals. Online listings are updated daily. Accounting and EDP professionals who wish to post to the candidate section must first submit their résumés for approval. All résumés are posted anonymously, and responses are coordinated though RJ Pascale. Contact the company at 500 Summer Street, Stamford, CT, 06901, attention: Mr. Joseph Yarsawich; fax: (203) 969-3990; e-mail: WY@Futuris.net.

Business Opportunities

BizOp, Business Opportunities Mailing List

To subscribe: bizbot@teletron.com

Message: subscribe

A free mailing list for announcing new business and/or self-employment opportunities, this list is very entrepreneurial in

* See also FinanceNet in Chapter 9.

nature. The mail flow is light with one to three messages a day. *Caveat emptor!* I saw a few strange things in this list like multilevel marketing schemes and "send two letters and you'll make thousands of dollars immediately" schemes! The list owner is Howard Barton; contact him at sysop@teletron.com.

Sales/Marketing

American Marketing Association

http://www.ama.org

This site offers a couple of different placement/referral services for a fee. It does not have a menu structure of any kind, so use the search engine to find resources.

Direct Marketing World Job Center

http: //mainsail.com/jobs.html

An electronic directory of the direct marketing industry, Direct Marketing provides a site where employers can list open positions, and job seekers can post their own résumés. This site is limited to business, but includes a very good selection of these types of jobs.

ELMAR—Researchers in Marketing Mailing List

To subscribe: elmar-request@columbia.edu

Message: SUBSCRIBE ELMAR-LIST or ELMAR-DIGEST (*please indicate which subscription you prefer*)

A moderated e-mail list for researchers in marketing. Although specific contents are determined by participants, the list will accept and post announcements of faculty positions or positions requiring a Ph. D. Postings containing résumés will be rejected. For more information, contact the list owner, Peter Palij, via e-mail at pbp1@columbia.edu.

> **Internet Tip: What's a digest?** Most mailing lists offer you the option of receiving a digest. This means that your mail from the list will be held until it reaches a certain number of postings or a certain file size. Instead of receiving 20 messages, you will receive one message with all 20 postings included. For some, this is an easier way to handle mail.

Quality Control

American Society for Quality Control

http: //www.asqc.org/

The American Society for Quality Control (ASQC) is the leading quality improvement organization in the United States, with more than 130,000 individual and 1,000 sustaining members worldwide. ASQC's *Personnel Listing Service*—a monthly publication in which companies and recruiters advertise position openings—is free to all members who request it. *Note*: There is a fee for membership, and membership is necessary to receive the job listings. For more information, call (800) 248-1946 (United States, Canada, and Mexico only) or (414) 272-8575.

CHAPTER 6

Jobs in Science, Engineering, Agriculture, Technology, and the Environment

The Internet resources in this chapter provide career information for the many fields of science and engineering, including jobs in computing and technology. Use the virtual libraries, the Internet indexers, and the Web search engines to locate additional employment opportunities not included here. Scholarly and professional societies also include leads to employment, so use the **Scholarly Societies Project** noted in **Chapter 3** to find these organizations. Don't forget **Usenet newsgroups** and **mailing lists** that discuss topics of interest in these fields, nor the more **academic job**-listing services which may also carry announcements of research positions with related organizations.

> **Job Search Tip:** Don't expect to find that dream job posted on the Internet: if it's a dream to you, it very well may be a dream to thousands of others. The true value of the Internet is as a source of information. Just as in traditional, nontechnical job-seeking methods, the keywords are "Networking" and "Information gathering." Tap into the wealth of information on the Internet and then use your people and self-marketing skills to do your follow-up.
> **Judy A. Carbone,** *Career Consultant, Career Development Center, George Mason University, Fairfax, VA.*

General Resources and Listings in Multiple Fields

American Indian Science & Engineering Society (AISESnet)

http://bioc02.uthscsa.edu/aisesnet.html

gopher://bioc02.uthscsa.edu/11/AISESnet%20Gopher

One of the services offered by AISESnet is a Gopher job database that provides information about internships and other kinds of positions in addition to science and engineering jobs. It also includes links to other resources for Native Americans. For more information, contact the society via e-mail at demeler @bioc02.uthscsa.edu.

CSUS Student/Alumni Employment Opportunities

gopher://gopher.csus.edu/11/employment

Maintained by the School of Engineering and Computer Science at California State University, Sacramento, this service has engineering and computer science job listings. Contact may be made by phone: (916) 278-7091; fax: (916) 278-5949; or e-mail: mattiuzzic@csus.edu.

Science JobNet, the American Association for the Advancement of Science

http://science-mag.aaas.org/science/

gopher://gopher.aaas.org:71/1

The global weekly magazine from the AAAS is now online, including the job listings in the Science JOBNET, the display classifieds (in JPEG format), and a main index arranged by agency or employer. The text and display classifieds are arranged in order of position type: faculty, postdoctoral, research associate, scientist, and general announcements. The current issue of the journal is online and updated the day of publication. The Web site is best viewed with a graphical browser for displaying the images, but text browsers can get around very well. AAAS is an excellent addition to the science listings and opportunitics online.

sci.research.careers

This newsgroup is for discussions about careers in the sciences and includes job postings.

sci.research.postdoc

A newsgroup for discussions among postdoctoral students about careers in the sciences, it includes job postings.

The Scientist (electronic journal)

gopher://ds.internic.net/1/pub/the-scientist

telnet ds.internic.net

login: gopher

Choose #2, 4, and 6, from successive menus

ftp: //ds.internic.net/pub/the-scientist

This is the text version of the print newspaper. It is biweekly and includes job listings for the United States, primarily, but not exclusively, in academic settings. Postdoctoral and research opportunities are also included. You can read either the entire online newspaper or just the classified ads/career opportunities, which are in separate files from the full text at the top of the menu. The most current edition is at the bottom of the list. If you have a problem accessing the file, send a message to garfield@aurora.cis.upenn.edu.

Young Scientist Network Electronic Newsletter

To subscribc: ysnadm@crow-t-robot.stanford.edu

message: subscribe yourfirstname yourlastname

This news digest is for discussing issues involving the employment of scientists, especially those just beginning their careers. The goals of this group, linked by computer e-mail, are to let the public know that there is currently no shortage of scientists and to discuss how young scientists can find both traditional and nontraditional careers. The information in the newsletter is very helpful to the job seeker, although it includes few job listings. Archives are included on its **Web server.** Created by Kevin Aylesworth of Cambridge, MA, the list is also managed by John Quackenbush of Stanford, CA. Contact Quackenbush by phone at (415) 812-1915, or fax at (415) 812-1916. Send e-mail to ysnadm@ crow-t-robot.stanford.edu. Phone Aylesworth at (617) 491-9872, or send e-mail to kda@pinet.aip.org.

Young Scientist Network Job and Grant Listings

Send e-mail to: ysn-joblist@atlas.chemistry.uakron.edu

*For jobs list, type **send** as the subject*

*For grants, type **grants** as the subject*

This server contains job openings that have been submitted to the Young Scientist Network (YSN). All relate to science or computers. Archives are available on the **YSN Web server or in its FTP site**. For more information, contact Mary Ellen Scott, University of Akron Chemistry Dept., Akron, OH 44325-3601; phone: (216) 972-8392; e-mail: mes@atlas.chemistry.uakron.edu.

Young Scientist Network Jobs Listings Archive

http: //www.physics.uiuc.edu/ysn

These URLs will take you directly to the archives of the job listings from the *YSN Job Listings Newsletter*, but the full newsletter can also be accessed at this site. You should examine the most recent three to four weeks of YSN postings for job ads, since there's a bit of a time-lag in getting them here. In addition to the listings, the archives feature articles on job searches, alternative careers, politics, and so forth. Great site for the young scientist!

Resources for Specific Fields

Aerospace/ Aviation

AV-Jobs

To subscribe: LISTSERV@rotor.com

Message: subscribe AV-Jobs your name

This mailing list carries job openings only, no résumés. All announcements cite the source of the listing, and many are from a newsletter called the *Airport Report*. Aviation aerospace listings are from all areas of the airline industry, with varying degrees of experience required. The site receives a moderate amount of mail. Contact the list owner, David Lutes, for more information at david.lutes@rotor.com.

Agriculture

Advanced Technology Information Network

http://www.atinet.org

http://caticsuf.csufresno.edu:70/1/atinet

ATIN hosts this listing of jobs in agriculture and with agriculture-related companies. It features six categories (management, sales and marketing, education, technology, research, and part time/seasonal/temporary) that can be scanned, or you can browse the list of all jobs posted. Call (209) 278-4872 for more information.

U.S. Dept of Agriculture—Cooperative Extension Job Vacancies

gopher: //sulaco.oes.orst.edu/11/ext/jobs

These employment vacancies in the U.S. Extension Services are provided courtesy of Oregon State University. Job openings, primarily for individuals in the sciences, agriculture, forestry, and academic fields, are in alphabetical order by state. For more information contact the Extension personnel office in your state. Connection problems? Contact helpdesk@oes.orst.edu or call (503) 727-4177.

U.S. Dept of Agriculture—Job Bank Bulletins

To subscribe: almanac@esuda.gov

Message: subscribe cite-jobs-mg

Provided by the Communications, Technology, and Distance Education Staff, Cooperative State Research, Education, and Extension Service of the U.S. Department of Agriculture, this service features agriculture-related jobs with universities or extension services. Most positions require research or management experience. For more information, contact the editor, Jodi Horigan, via e-mail at jhorigan@esusda.gov.

Architecture

CLRNet Architecture and Land Architecture Jobs

http: //www.clr.toronto.edu/VIRTUALLIB/jobs.html

The Centre for Landscape Research Network lists professional and academic positions in architecture and landscape architecture. This site is maintained by the School of Architecture and Landscape Architecture at the University of Toronto. It includes links to other related sources of information and employment resources, including Deb Sommers' *Architecture Job Hunt Guide* **(UC Berkeley)** and information on **GIS Jobs** (*see separate listings*). Contact rodney@clr.toronto.edu.

Artificial Intelligence

AI-Jobs

To subscribe: ai+query@cs.cmu.edu

AI-Jobs exists to help programmers and researchers find positions, and to help companies find programmers and researchers. Jobs available in the artificial intelligence field are e-mailed to subscribers each week. Contact Mark Kantrowitz via e-mail at Mark.Kantrowitz@GLINDA.OZ.CS.CMU.EDU.

Astronomy

American Astronomical Society Job Register

http: //www.aas.org/JobRegister/aasjobs.html

The American Astronomical Society (AAS) is the major professional organization in North America for astronomers and other scientists and individuals interested in astronomy. The AAS Job Register lists positions available in the field of astronomy. The AAS requires that all employment advertisers submit an accompanying statement assuring that the vacancy being listed is bona fide and the position has not been promised to anyone. Contact the AAS via regular mail at 2000 Florida Avenue, Suite 400, Washington, DC 20009; phone: (202) 328-2010; fax: (202) 234-2560; membership fax: (202) 588-1351); e-mail: aas@aas.org.

Biology/ Biotechnology/ Physiology

American Physiological Association

gopher: //oac.hsc.uth.tmc.edu:3300/11/employ

This Gopher site lists jobs in physiology.

BIO Online

http: //www.bio.com

A comprehensive site for biotechnology-related information and services on the Internet, BIO Online combines resources from biotechnology companies, biotechnology centers, research and academic institutions, industry suppliers, government agencies, and nonprofit special-interest groups. This site is maintained by the Biotechnology Industry Organization (BIO) and Vitadata Corporation. The Career Center includes employment postings, career guides, and a link to a search firm working in the biotechnology industry. You can search job listings by keyword or examine the list of employers for opportunities. Note that some of these positions are administrative and may not require a background in biotechnology.

bionet.jobs.offered

This newsgroup lists job openings in the biological sciences or professional-level jobs that support biological scientists. Commercial positions may be listed here using the guidelines specified.

bionet.jobs.wanted

This newsgroup posts résumés and requests from persons looking for work and research opportunities in biological fields.

bit.listserv.biojobs

This newsgroup duplicates the postings in the Biojobs mailing list.

BioSci Employment Opportunities
http://www.bio.net/hypermail/EMPLOYMENT

BioSci Employment Wanted
http://www.bio.net/hypermail/EMPLOYMENT-WANTED

These are the archives of the Bionet newsgroups. Check the "Current" files for the most recent listings.

BMEnet
http://bme.www.ecn.purdue.edu/bme

The Biomedical Engineering net (BMEnet) maintained by Purdue University provides links to several Gopher servers with job information: jobs listed by BME (mostly academic positions), *Science* magazine job postings in biomedical engineering, National Institutes of Health, Career Center, and many others.

European Molecular Biology Lab, Heidelberg, Germany
http: //www.embl-heidelberg.de/ExternalInfo/jobs/

The European Molecular Biology Lab (EMBL) provides a listing of jobs available at the lab. These jobs are normally offered to Europeans.

Franklin Search Group Online
http://www.chemistry.com/biotech-jobs/

The Franklin Search Group (FSG) recruits for the biotech, pharmaceutical, and medical industries. Candidates and employers can post and search résumés and positions, and obtain complete contact information at no charge. A salary guide is also available along with a list of job hotline numbers for a selection of companies. Please register as a guest to let the group know who is using this service. For general information, send e-mail to info-biotech-jobs@gate.net; or contact Dr. Frank Heasley, President, Franklin Search Group, Inc. by fax at (305) 434-4840; e-mail: fheasley@chemistry.com.

Hum-Molgen Bioscience and Medicine

http://www.informatik.uni-rostock.de/HUM-MOLGEN/anno/position.html

Users can announce positions in bioscience and medicine. Announcements are searchable by type of position, keyword, subject, and continent. Positions are categorized as "Postdocs or Research Associates," "Assistant or Associate Professors," "Higher Academic Positions," or "Clinical Positions."

Chemistry

Academic Chemical Employment Clearinghouse

http://hackberry.chem.niu.edu:70/1/ChemJob

A service of Northern Illinois University, there are not many listings here currently, but it is one of the very few with chemistry offerings. Listings are divided into analytical, biochemical, inorganic, organic, and physical chemistry.

Computing and Technology

Because of the amount of information available, we've divided this section into several categories covering general resources, professional societies, recruiters, and other agencies.

General Resources

The Ada Project (TAP)

http://www.cs.yale.edu/HTML/YALE/CS/HyPlans/tap/positions.html

TAP is intended to be a collection of resources for women in computing, but most links and listed resources are gender neutral and useful to anyone in need of information.

CIS-L—Careers Information Systems Mailing List

To subscribe: listserv@ube.ubalt.edu

Message: subscribe CIS-L yourfirstname yourlastname

CIS-L is an unmoderated discussion list for anyone interested in trends, opportunities, and changes in careers in information systems (IS). Although CIS-L is primarily intended for professors of information systems, it invites the participation of IS managers and consultants, and human resources managers and professors interested in IS careers. Authors of CIS-L messages are solely responsible for their content. For more information, send e-mail to the list owner, Al Bento, at earvaben@ube.ubalt.edu.

comp.jobs.offered

This newsgroup features job openings in computing and technology.

ComputerWorld's Career Center

http: //careers. computerworld.com

ComputerWorld magazine is a leading industry journal for computing and information technology. This site contains online copies of various articles from the weekly magazine on career-related subjects and job listings arranged by recruiting company. Additional information on careers in computing and upcoming job fairs is included.

Computist's Communique

To subscribe: LAWS@ai.sri.com

The Computist's Communique is a news service of Computist's International. Forty-four weekly issues include journal calls, National Science Foundation announcements, grant and research news, online resources, and business tips, plus current topics and tips from Internet discussion groups—a concise, time-saving summary from dozens of sources! Each issue also has a less condensed weekly online digest, **Applied Jobs Digest (APJ)**. The APJ is recommended for job seekers and the *Communique* looks very worthwhile, too. Dues are $115 for professionals, $45 for students (or those with equivalent salaries), and free for unemployed software scientists. Members outside the United States get a 50 percent discount, and renewals may also qualify for 20 percent off. For more information, contact Dr. Kenneth I. Laws by e-mail at laws@ai.sri.com, or by phone at (415) 493-7390.

HPCWire BULLETIN

For job information, send e-mail to more@hpcwire.ans.net.

In the subject field, type: 667 (to receive job listings)

Do not place any text in the body of the message.

This is a text-on-demand news magazine for high-performance computing. A full subscription with access to all the news stories requires a paid subscription, but limited access to news, the bulletin, and job announcements is free. You can retrieve the job bank listings and get information on adding listings at no charge. For a free trial subscription, send e-mail to trial@hpcwire.ans.net.

Recruiters

D.I.C.E., Data Processing Independent Consultant's Exchange

telnet dice.com (*best access*)
login as "new" (no quotation marks)

http://www.dice.com

ftp://dice.com

D.I.C.E. is a free service for high-tech professionals looking for detailed information on consulting and full-time positions. D.I.C.E. is *not* a placement agency; it is an electronic job-advertisement service. Most positions posted here are in data processing, engineering, or technical writing. The Web and FTP sites have just been added, and they are not yet as interactive and easy to use as the Telnet link. Notice that D.I.C.E. goes offline to post new jobs three times a day. The times are posted on the site.

DXI Corporation, Atlanta, GA

http://isotropic.com/dxicorp/dxihome.html

DXI Corporation, founded in 1981, provides services to the information processing industry. It utilizes consultants for this work, and its clients include many Fortune 500 companies as well as many smaller technology companies. DXI has a list of specialties for which it is currently recruiting, including technical writing, and résumés can be e-mailed or faxed to the company.

Enterprise's 1-800-NETWORK

http://www.enterprise.skill.com/

If you work in client/server applications, this is a good place for you to look. Enterprise specializes in finding the experts and placing them in jobs all over the United States. To view job opportunities, you select a city and the contact information for that location is at the top of the file. You can submit your résumé via e-mail or by calling (800) NETWORK. This site also connects to two other interesting services, one for Macintosh specialists and one for freelancers in graphic design.

The Job Board, Jason Smith's TechnoCycle

http://www.io.org/~jwsmith/jobs.html

This recruiter for hi-tech positions has new job openings listed at the top of the file.

JobLink

http://joblink.com/joblink.html

JobLink lists technical positions and information on member companies. Individuals can apply directly for positions via electronic link or to the addresses provided. Options include searching for a job by geographic location (zip code or city), required skill (keyword and length of time), company name, or any combination thereof. Candidates can leave their résumés in a "general area" also. If your browser does not support forms, you can look at the job listings for each company. For more information, send e-mail to jackie@msc.com.

MacTemps

http://www.mactemps.com/

MacTemps features jobs in office support, graphic design, or training. Most jobs listed are permanent (not temporary). Contact Sarah Edgcomb by phone at (617) 868-8200; fax: (617) 868-6104; e-mail: sedgcomb@mactemps.com; or regular mail: 66 Church Street, Cambridge, MA 02138.

NTES—National Technical Employment Services

http: //iquest.com/~ntes

National Technical Employment Services was founded in 1983 to assist contract professionals in obtaining assignments. Contract jobs in all disciplines are updated daily. The information here is very brief—just the job title, a quick list of skills, and the date the position was posted. You must contact the recruiting company for more information. The best list is the New HOTFLASH consisting of jobs posted during the past week. Check out the Contract Employment FAQ and Recruiters Online and How to Contact Them at info@ntes.com for e-mail or phone (205) 259-2272.

PENCOM Career Center

http: //www.pencomsi.com

Pencom is a national multifaceted software services company specializing in open systems technology and providing full-time placement, contract programming, systems, administration, and software development. This site includes job listings and a place you can put your résumé at no cost. It also has a unique *interactive salary survey* to develop your worth based on years of experience, specific skills, and so forth. I highly recommend that computer professionals check out the salary survey. Contact Judy Cohen by voice mail at (212) 513-7777; fax: (212) 227-1854; e-mail: judy@pencom.com; or regular mail: 40 Fulton Street New York, NY 10038-1850.

Provident Search Group

http: //www.dpjobs.com/

The Provident Search Group, Inc. has been placing data processing professionals with Fortune 500 companies since 1979. All fees are paid by the hiring company, and applicants have no contractual obligation. Job listings are arranged by specialty, and you will have to contact the office for more information. New jobs are posted as they arrive, and companies may have other positions besides these listings. An 800 number is available for phone and fax inquiries: (800) 626-8808.

SDC Computer Services, Inc.

http: //www.windowware.com/sdc/index.html

SDC Computer Services, Inc. specializes in the contracting and permanent placement of information management and systems technology professionals. Based in Kirkland, WA, it has 24 offices nationwide and keeps over 150,000 résumés in its database. Résumés can be faxed or e-mailed, or you can call and speak with a representative. There is no fee for services to job seekers. Contact SDC at SDCNW@Halcyon.Com.

Transaction Information Systems (TIS)

http://www.tisny.com/

High-tech recruiters post their Hot Jobs on the Web server every week. TIS accepts résumés via e-mail for both posting and applying for listed positions.

Westech Career Expo Virtual Job Fair

http://www.careerexpo.com/

Westech Career Expo offers a variety of resources for the technical professional (computer, engineering, technical related), including job opportunities, links to employing organizations, and a technical career magazine. For information, send e-mail to editor@careerexpo.com.

Western Technical Resources

http://www.webcom.com/~wtr/

Western Technical Resources maintains a daily updated list of open temporary and career technical positions for its clientele. Job seekers select from listed opportunities, enter job search preferences and skill sets, then paste their résumé with a forms-capable browser such as Netscape. A confirmation is sent to clients via e-mail almost immediately.

Professional Societies

ACM SIGMOD

http://bunny.cs.uiuc.edu/jobs/

The Association for Computing Machinery's Special Interest Group on Management of Data (ACM SIGMOD) includes job announcements on its information server. Announcements are filed under date received and are not necessarily deleted when the search is closed. The most recent month of announcements is at the top of the file.

Computing Research Association

http://cra.org/jobs

ftp: //cra.org

listproc@cra.org

Message: subscribe CRA

The Computing Research Association (CRA) is an association of North American academic computer science and computer engineering departments, industrial labs, and professional societies. Its job listings are text files only, but the location and date of posting can be gleaned from the file name. Be sure to check the job listing dates for currency. The mailing list features job announcements for computer science faculty, and archives are available at the FTP site. Contact CRA via e-mail at josuna@cra.org.

Institute of Electrical and Electronic Engineers (IEEE) Job Bank

http://www.ieee.org/jobs.html

Located on the main information server for the IEEE, the Job Bank divides its postings into six geographical regions within the United States and has a separate listing for jobs in other countries. Hundreds of jobs are listed at this location, and the fee for employers to list here is nominal. The Institute of Electrical and Electronic Engineers is a key professional organization in the field, and this is a valuable source of on-line information.

IEEE Computer Society

http://www.computer.org/pubs/computer/career/career.htm

Career information is posted here by the computer section of the IEEE. These are the current job announcements from *Computer*, the monthly journal for this section of the IEEE.

IEEE, University of Massachusetts Student Branch

http: //www.ecs.umass.edu/ieeesb/index.html

The University of Massachusetts provides excellent links to the IEEE homepages (where the jobs are listed), newsgroups, and services for electronic engineers. For more information, call (413) 545-0641 or send e-mail to ieeesb@kira.ecs.umass.edu.

Other Organizations

CERL Sound Group

http: //datura.cerl.uiuc.edu/netStuff/jobs/jobs.html

The CERL Sound Group is a center for research and hardware/ software development in digital audio signal processing, and it has a unique presence in the world of computer music, sound computation, and digital audio signal processing. The group works with experts in electrical and computer engineering, computer science, and music. Job listings here are a mix of programming and technological research for music and audio work and call for composers and experts in computer and electronic music, including many faculty positions at well-known schools of music around the world. For more information, contact the CERL Sound Group, 252 Engineering Research Laboratory, 103 South Mathews Street, Urbana, IL 61801-2977; phone: (217) 333-0766; e-mail: sound@cerl.uiuc.edu.

Instructional Technology Jobs, Indiana University, Bloomington

http: //education.indiana.edu/ist/students/jobs/joblink.html

This site has five categories of listings, but nothing has been updated since 1994 except for the "Current Openings Just Received," which is apparently being updated by a MailBot. You will have to scroll past several old listings to get to the newest ones, which are at the bottom of the file.

SPAWAR—Headquarters Space and Naval Command Warfare Center

http: //dolomite.spawar.navy.mil/

Part of "Navy Online," this is the place for all young pre-teen warriors...or anyone looking for a little adventure from their desktop! See a virtual demonstration of laser space warfare complete with battle sounds and animation. The SPAWAR corporate telephone directory is available to identify every corporation involved and can be downloaded with links. You then have an electronic phone book on hand whenever you need it, with the benefit of keyword/hypertext searches and the added flexibility of copy and paste commands at your workstation. This is useful for job seekers interested in high-tech defense opportunities. It also features an excellent section on diversity. Send your questions via e-mail to Webserver@smtp-gw.spawar.navy.mil.

vmsnet.employment

This moderated newsgroup lists job announcements for DEC VAX/VMS and DECNET computer systems users.

Crystallography

Employment in Crystallography

http://www.unige.ch/crystal/w3vlc/job-index.html

A central site for job listings in this field, jobs are listed by category—faculty, postdoctoral, and so on. You can also examine the jobs by geographic location. Links are provided to two other databases with jobs in this field.

Engineering Education

American Society for Engineering Education (ASEE)

http://www.asee.org/asee/publications/prism/classifieds/

These classified ads are posted online 30 days before their publication in the *ASEE PRISM* journal. All types of positions in educational institutions and college/university administration in engineering schools are included here.

Entomology

Job Opportunities in Entomology

http: //www.colostate.edu/Depts/Entomology/jobs/jobs.html

L.B. Bjostad and J.K. VanDyk at Colorado State University update this listing of jobs and fellowships in entomology. For more information, send e-mail to lbjostad@lamar.colostate.edu.

Environment/ Ecology

EE-Link: The Environmental Education Gopher Server

gopher: //nceet.snre.umich.edu/11/networking/

telnet nceet.snre.umich.edu

login: eelink

These job listings in environmental education and studies include several internships. The main server has a tremendous amount of information for individuals in this field.

ENVENG-L—Environmental Engineering Mailing List

To subscribe: listproc@pan.cedar.univie.ac.at

Message: subscribe enveng-1

ENVENG-L serves as a communications medium for those interested in education, research, and the professional practice of environmental engineering. Topics encompass the entire field, including water and wastewater treatment, air pollution control, solid waste management, and radioactive waste treatment. Job postings may be submitted for listing, but please do not post résumés here. For more information, contact the list owner, Charles N.Haas, via e-mail at HaasCN@Dunx 1.ocs.drexel.edu.

Virginia Coast Reserve Information System (VCRIS) (Job Listings)

gopher: //atlantic.evsc.Virginia.EDU/11/Opportunities

http: //atlantic.evsc.virginia.edu

Job and internship opportunities in ecological research and studies are available here. On the Gopher, the best listings are in the Jobs directory, but you will need to read the listing to find the date of posting, and so on. There is some very old information here, but it appears that the newest listings are at the end.

Geographic Information Systems (GIS)

GIS-JOBS

To subscribe: gis-jobs-request@MAILBASE.AC.UK

This mailing list features job announcements in the geographic information systems (GIS) field, mostly in the United Kingdom.

GIS Jobs Clearinghouse

http://www.gis.umn.edu/rsgisinfo/jobs.html

ftp://torpedo.gis.umn.edu/pub/gisjobs

The Remote Sensing Lab at the University of Minnesota maintains this site featuring positions throughout the United States in geographic information systems (GIS), global positioning systems (GPS), and image processing (IP). Four months of job announcements are on the Web page, with archives available by month in the FTP site. There is a search index for both the Web and Gopher sites. At the time of review, the clearinghouse had a notice that the Gopher was being dismantled but the Web address may change in the near future. For more information, contact jobs-info@torpedo.gis.umn.edu or sdlime@torpedo.forestry.umn.edu.

Geosciences

GEOSCI-JOBS

To subscribe: listserv@netcom.com

Message: subscribe GEOSCI-JOBS your e-mail address

GEOSCI-JOBS is a moderated listserv for postings of employment opportunities in the geosciences, including geology, geophysics, seismology, engineering geology, geological engineering, civil engineering, paleontology, petroleum geology, and so forth. Research, postdoctoral opportunities, and internship information is also posted here; no résumés please. It has a moderate mail flow. Contact Ted Smith at ted.smith@mtnswest.com or tcsmith@netcom.com.

Mathematics

American Mathematical Society

http://www.ams.org/committee/profession/employ.html

The American Mathematical Society (AMS) provides a fantastic service, including lists of employment and postdoctoral opportunities for mathematicians, instructions for posting your résumé, and articles on careers in mathematics. If you can take the time, read the report on the AMS study to find more careers for professionals in mathematics.

Materials/ Minerals/Metals

JOM, The Minerals, Metals, and Materials Society Journal

http://www.tms.org/pubs/journals/JOM/classifieds.html

Employment opportunities for specialists in materials, minerals, and metals are listed as they appear in *JOM*. Only the "Positions Available" from the most recent issues are included. Most positions are academic or research oriented, but many include corporate opportunities and needs.

Medical/Health Sciences

Academic Physician and Scientist

gopher://aps.acad-phy-sci.com/

A joint effort of Academic Physician and Scientist and the Association of American Medical Colleges (AAMC), this Gopher server lists academic medical teaching positions for the 126 U.S. medical schools and their affiliated institutions. Openings are listed categorically by specialty and state. The service is free of charge and includes job opportunities with the FDA and NIH.

Hospital.Net

http://hospital.net

Hospital.Net formed to help hospitals, doctors, patients, and families communicate using the Internet. It is primarily intended for medical professionals and is very comprehensive. With some diligence, a job seeker can unearth some job listings, and Hospital.Net is a good starting point for learning about and networking within the medical field. The media contact is Linda Burnett; phone: (212) 799-2645; fax: (212) 799-1075; e-mail: info@hospital.net for more information.

Hospital Web

http://132.183.145.103/hospitalweb.html

Hospital Web features over 100 hospital Web pages, some of which include job listings. It is maintained by John Lester of the Department of Neurology at Massachusetts General Hospital. He can be contacted at lester@helix.mgh.harvard.edu.

MedLink International

http://www.medlink.com/opps/opps.html

Physician employment listings, primarily in the United States, are divided by region (northeast, northwest, southeast, southwest) and specialty. Employers' identities are blocked, and all inquiries must be directed to MedLink. Posting dates for positions are not given. Curriculum vitae may be posted here.

MedSearch America

http://www.medsearch.com/

gopher://gopher.medsearch.com

MedSearch recruits for the medical community and related health care and biotechnology positions. It also maintains a résumé bank for medical and health services professionals. If you have e-mail access, there is no charge for sending your résumé. Those without Internet access can also post their résumés, but must submit them through U.S. mail with a small fee for inclusion in the database.

Nightingale, University of Tennessee—Knoxville

gopher://nightingale.con.utk.edu/11/communications/Positions

Nursing positions and pointers to more information are provided by the University of Tennessee at Knoxville.

Nurse

http://www.csv.warwick.ac.uk: 8000/jobs.html

gopher://nurse.csv.warwick.ac.uk/11/jobs

These job listings and resources for nurses are maintained at the University of Warwick in the United Kingdom, but are not limited to U.K. jobs. Nurse includes links to other resources for jobs in medical and health care industries.

Nursing Career Opportunities

gopher: //umabnet.ab.umd.edu/11/.schools/.nursing

The School of Nursing at the University of Maryland at Baltimore maintains this Gopher site featuring job postings for nursing faculty, administration, and other positions. Contact Dr. Elizabeth Rankin via e-mail at rankin@nurse-1.ab.umd.edu.

Physicians Employment

http: //www.fairfield.com/physemp/index.html

This site has job listings for physicians in all specialties. The form asks for your name, e-mail address, phone number, specialty, and preferred location, but access to the listings can be had without filling in all of the spaces. Listings are arranged by specialty, and notes show the last time a file was added to. Military positions are included, and if your specialty is not listed, you can send in a form requesting referrals. Great site!

Meteorology, Climatology, and Atmospheric Science

MET-JOBS—Jobs in Meteorology, Climatology, and Atmospheric Sciences

To subscribe: listserv@netcom.com

Message: subscribe MET-JOBS your e-mail address

Formerly included with the GEOSCI-JOBS mailing list, these announcements of meteorology, climatology, and atmospheric science positions now have their own list.

Natural Resources and Water Resources

Employment Opportunities in Water-Resources

http://www.uwin.siu.edu/announce

The University Water Information Network provides this "...clearinghouse for jobs and related opportunities in various water resources fields." It includes positions throughout the United States. For more information, contact Faye Anderson via e-mail at faye@uwin.siu.edu, or by fax at (618) 453-2671.

Jobs in Natural Resources

http: //www.environment.sfasu.edu:1080/topics/jobs.html

The College of Forestry at Stephen F. Austin State University provides this site with links to job opportunities in natural resources. Send e-mail to z_hiltoncc@titan.sfasu.edu for more information.

Optical Engineering

OPTOLINK, from SPIE

http://www.spie.org/web/employment/employ_home.html

telnet spie.org

login: OPTOLINK, **password:** GUEST

SPIE, the International Society for Optical Engineering, is a non-profit professional association dedicated to advancing research and applications in the optical sciences. The job opportunities taken from SPIE's monthly newspaper, *OE Reports*, are separated into four different categories: candidates with Ph.D.s, those with M.S. degrees, those with B.S. and other degrees, and "Consultants." There is also a "Positions Wanted" section to help employers in the industry find qualified candidates. Contact the society by phone at (360) 676-3290 or fax at (360) 647-1445.

Physics

hepnet.jobs

This newsgroup posts jobs within the High Energy and Nuclear Physics network.

AIPJOBS, The American Institute of Physics Employment Opportunities Database

telnet pinet.aip.org

login: aipjobs, **password:** aipjobs

You will need to register using your first and last name and your e-mail address to access AIPJOBS, although membership is not required. For more information, send e-mail to cpp@aip.org.

Physics Job Announcements by Thread

http://XXX.lanl.gov/Announce/Jobs/

Provided by Los Alamos National Laboratory, this is a great list of mostly higher-level positions at all kinds of universities and research labs. When we checked the site, all the jobs were for postdoctorates, lectureships, or faculty. Contact the site via e-mail at www-admin@xxx.lanl.gov.

Physics Around the World

http://www.physics.mcgill.ca/deptdocs/physics_services.html

The initial index structure is very general (you must use the search engine to get listings), but it has great stuff! Using the **keywords "job, employment,"** an initial search yielded a *wide* variety of physics jobs of all kinds in industry and research/education that were international in scope. *Caution*: This listing is maintained by a graduate student on a volunteer basis, but it seems to be current and very well maintained with great graphics and well-done links. It is maintained by the Physics Dept. at McGill University, Canada (Mikko Karttunen—karttune@physics.mcgill.ca) and the Technical University of Vienna (Gunther Nowotny).

Physics World Jobs Online

http://www.iop.org/Mags/PWJOBS/index.html

To subscribe: listproc@listerver.ioppublishing.com

Message: subscribe PWJOBS your name

International jobs in physics, but mostly in England, are listed here. Each issue's ads are posted separately, and back issues are on the server. Most ads appear to be international. You can also receive these announcements via e-mail by using the listproc address above. Contact the Institute of Physics Publishing (U.K.) for more information.

Statistics

University of Florida Department of Statistics

http://www.stat.ufl.edu/users/bonnie/JobAnnouncements.html

This Internet address goes directly to the Statistics Department's list of nationwide job openings for both academic and business statistics candidates.

CHAPTER 7

Jobs in Academe and the Arts and Humanities

Academe is well represented online and has been for a long time. Colleges and universities all over the world are establishing online information servers and including their open positions as a recruiting tool. Jobs in the arts and humanities are thought to be unavailable online. I think we have managed to produce a few interesting and creative answers to that challenge, and your creativity can probably produce even more.

Job Search Tip: The term "cover letter" is a misnomer and therefore very misleading to job applicants who think all they have to write is two or three lines saying that they are applying for a job and their résumé or curriculum vitae (CV) is attached. Such a letter, as part of the application package, should more rightly be referred to as an *application letter*. Employers expect applicants to "sell themselves," that is, to match themselves to the qualifications, qualities, and skills required for the position, as well as to include their résumé or CV. This is expected both electronically and through the mail. With the growth of résumé-writing and typing consultants, the résumé is becoming secondary in the application procedure. Many employers are now relying on the application letter to show them the "real" applicant, because most people still feel comfortable and confident enough to write their own letters.
Susan Akers, *Careers Officer, Northern Territory University, Darwin, Australia*

Academe

These are opportunities for teaching and research positions with colleges and universities all around the world. Job listings for K–12 have been included in the **education** section in **Chapter 8**. Individual colleges and universities, which can be located easily using the resources noted in **Chapter 3**, are not included here.

Academe This Week

http://chronicle.merit.edu/.ads/.links.html

gopher://chronicle.merit.edu/11/.ads

The current job listings from *The Chronicle of Higher Education*, the weekly newspaper of higher education, are online every Tuesday afternoon, a day before the print publication is released. Listings can be searched by geographic location, the Chronicle's list of job terms, or keywords of your own choosing. Only the current week's listings are maintained, and all old listings are deleted. This is the best source for academic and research positions with U.S. colleges and universities, and many international institutions and companies with research divisions advertise here also.

Academic Position Network (APN)

gopher://wcni.cis.umn.edu:11111

The Academic Position Network (APN) is an online position announcement service for academic institutions all over the world. Job listings include faculty, administration, and staff positions, as well as announcements for research fellowships and graduate assistantships. The APN files may be browsed as they are organized: by country, state, or institution. The entire text may be searched using a word or combination of words separated by "and" or "or."

Job Search Tip: Looking for Work in Academe. If you are interested in teaching at a college or university, you can check an institution's Web and Gopher servers to look for job listings, including assistantships, fellowships, and postdoctoral opportunities. Use **The Mother Gopher** and **The Master List of WWW Servers** to look for institutions in various areas, and then look for their human resources departments and even the specific department you are interested in. Professional societies may also carry good announcements. If you are looking for an institution with a particular specialty, use **virtual libraries** to target departments.

CAUSE Job Posting Service

http://cause-www.colorado.edu/pd/jobpost/jobpost.html

gopher://cause-gopher.colorado.edu/11/job-post

CAUSE is the association for managing and using information resources in higher education. Its membership includes network administrators, librarians, and chief information officers (CIOs) for academic institutions all over the world. The CAUSE Job Posting Service allows member organizations to post job openings. It can be browsed or searched by job type or region, including Canada and international. Positions for information managers, CIOs, directors of information systems, technical support personnel, and even some librarians were included at the time of review. Positions are removed on the date of closing. Contact the service by phone: (303) 449-4430; fax: (303) 440-0461; or e-mail: info@cause.colorado.edu.

Council for the Support and Advancement of Education (CASE) Job Classifieds

gopher://gopher.case.org:70/11/currents

Specializing in administrative positions in academe and education, these jobs might be listed elsewhere, such as in *The Chronicle of Higher Education*. The list is well maintained.

NISS, National Information Services and Systems

http://www.niss.ac.uk/news/index.html#jobs

telnet niss.ac.uk

select AB

select 7, Job Vacancies.

This list includes employment opportunities at the many universities in the Commonwealth countries (England, Canada, Australia, India, and so on). There are several fields listed, and links to additional job resources for these areas are also included.

The Times Higher Education Supplement InterView

http://www.timeshigher.newsint.co.uk/INTERVIEW/interview.html

gopher://caxton.co.uk/11/

The InterView service is the fastest way to finding jobs in higher education. Jobs are updated every Tuesday at 3 P.M., with the ads booked to appear in the following Friday's print edition of *The Times Higher Education Supplement*. InterView carries lists from all categories of higher-education job vacancies worldwide as advertised in *The Times*. Jobs are sorted into U.K. or international groups and then sorted by their classification type, that is, lecturers and tutors, principal/senior lecturers, professors, and readers and chairs. Listings are retained for about one month or until filled, whichever comes first. This is a great resource for U.K. educational postings. The Web page links back to the Gopher.

University of Minnesota's College of Education Job Search Bulletin Board

gopher://rodent.cis.umn.edu:11119/

Administrative, K–12, and higher education jobs of all kinds are arranged by broad areas. The location of the positions is included in the menu, so you can look for those close to you or in specific areas.

Arts and Humanities

Opportunities for employment in the arts and humanities are not easily found on the Internet, but they are there. As a job seeker, you should first discover what your options are based on what you like to do and what interests you, and then use your training to help you find the career path that will best fit these criteria. Remember that job listings might not come right out and state that a degree in English or art is necessary. You need to know where the skills and training you have will fit in! Examine the **job listing sites** in **Chapter 4** for more leads and use your creativity to explore the options.

General Information

The Arts Deadlines List

http://www.ircam.fr/divers/arts-deadlines.html

This server lists "competitions, contests, calls for entries/papers, grants, scholarships, fellowships, jobs, internships, etc. in the arts or related areas (painting, drawing, photography, etc.)." The list is also available by mail with a subscription. Contact Richard Gardner for more information via e-mail at rgardner@ charon.mit.edu.

Arts Wire Current

http://www.tmn.com/Artswire/

Arts Wire is a national computer-based communications network for the arts community. It is designed to enable artists, individuals, and organizations in arts communities across the country to better communicate, share information, and coordinate their activities. Arts Wire has several job listings in every issue. *Note:* There is an $18-per-month fee for unlimited access for individuals, or $20 per month for organizations. The "Arts Wire Current" (formerly Hotwire) section is accessible for free and lists a few jobs. To receive more information and a registration packet contact Judy Malloy, Arts Wire Front Desk Coordinator, 1502 Francis, Albany, CA 94796; phone: (510) 526-3993;e-mail: artswire@tmn.com.

Graphics Arts

3DSite

http://www.lightside.com/~dani/cgi/offers/index.html

The 3DSite is a server dedicated to three-dimensional computer graphics. The job list contains information on opportunities all over the world. These are arranged alphabetically by country, with the organization that is recruiting clearly noted. Postings are e-mailed to the owner every 30 days for updates. Note that not all of these positions require you to know programming languages! Many organizations are looking for talented artists who can use computers. A résumé database is available to which you can add your information. The database is accessed at http://www.lightside.com/~dani/.

GWeb, An Electronic Trade Journal for Computer Animators

http://www2.cinenet.net/GWEB/lists.html

GWeb has a great listing for those seeking work in computer animation. Jobs are listed by the company that is hiring, but they look great. Announcements are dated so you know when they were posted, and contact information is included.

Music and Audio

CERL Sound Group

http://datura.cerl.uiuc.edu/netStuff/jobs.html

The CERL Sound Group is a center for research and hardware/software development in digital audio signal processing, and it has a unique presence in the world of computer music, sound computation, and digital audio signal processing. The group works with experts in electrical and computer engineering, computer science, and music. Job listings here are a mix of programming and technological research for music and audio work and call for composers and experts in computer and electronic music, including many faculty positions at well-known schools of music around the world. For more information, contact the CERL Sound Group, 252 Engineering Research Laboratory, 103 South Mathews Street, Urbana, ILL 61801-2977; phone: (217) 333-0766; e-mail: sound@cerl.uiuc.edu.

ORCHESTRALIST

To subscribe: listproc@hubcap.clemson.edu

Message: subscribe orchestralist

ORCHESTRALIST is an unmoderated mailing list devoted to matters orchestral, and specifically designed for the orchestra professional. It serves as a forum to discuss such matters as orchestral repertoire, performance questions, conducting techniques, auditions, job opportunities (both professional and academic), marketing, organization, and other subjects. *Note:* This list is *not* a forum for discussion of recordings, anecdotes about conductors, and so on. There are other forums devoted to these topics. Although there are not many job listings, this list is a very active discussion group and a good way for orchestra professionals to network. For more information, contact Dr. Andrew

Levin, Assistant Professor of Music and conductor, Clemson University, South Carolina & Clemson University Chamber Orchestra via e-mail at aleven@hubcap.clemson.edu.

Journalism and Broadcast Media

Airwaves Job Services

http://radio.aiss.uiuc.edu/~rrb/job.html

Airwaves Media Page began as an outgrowth of *Airwaves Radio Journal* (ARJ) an interactive "Cyberzine" dedicated to domestic radio broadcasting. *ARJ* has been serving the Internet with professional-level radio discussion since 1991, as an e-mail reflector of the Usenet newsgroup **rec.radio.broadcasting**, which continues to be the place for radio professionals and serious nonprofessionals to meet and talk in a friendly and noise-free environment. The job site is a new addition to the Web server and is a varied listing of all kinds of work in the radio broadcast industry. You can also post positions wanted at this site. While you are here, visit the Master Web Page at http://radio.aiss.uiuc.edu/~rrb and let William Pfeiffer know how much you appreciate this service.

Job Openings in Newspaper New Media (and Related Fields)

http://www.mediainfo.com/edpub/ep/classi.html

Editor and Publisher Interactive provides positions listed in "new media," including journalism and online journalism-related positions. There are some technical-related jobs as well. For more information, contact outings@netcom.com

Video Production

VideoPro Classifieds

http://www.txdirect.net:80/videopro/adv.htm

VideoPro is a directory of video production professionals and services. The opportunities in video production range from graphics designer to videographer to equipment maintenance engineer. Posting dates are included, along with contact information for applications.

CHAPTER 8

Jobs in the Social Sciences and the World of Nonprofits

For convenience, we have grouped together two categories: the social sciences and non-profit agencies. For more leads to job listings, find resources in your field by using virtual libraries, Internet indexes, and search engines. Colleges and universities with good programs in your field may also collect employment leads or link to other helpful resources, as do many professional associations. Check the resources listed in **Chapter 4** for some other places to start your search.

Job Search Tip: If you see an ad and it says "mail to human resources," call and get the name for the head of the department where the job is and send that person a copy as well. I found that through my own job search, it was those letters that got me the interviews. It's an extra step and double the postage, but well worth it. **Angela Dunn**, *Career Counselor, Framingham State College, MA*

Nonprofit/Not-for-Profit

Opportunities with the many nonprofit organizations are not easy to locate. We have provided you with information to help you locate and contact these organizations rather than a collection of resources for employment opportunities.

Impact Online

http://www.webcom.com/~iol

Impact Online is a new nonprofit organization that helps people get involved with nonprofits nationwide through the use of technology. Impact educates, informs, and provides guidance to those interested in volunteering. This well-designed and informative site also features a directory (http://infobase.internex.net:80/impact/10nplist.html). For more information, send e-mail to impactol@aol.com.

International Service Agencies

http://www.charity.org/

The International Service Agencies' (ISA's) stated mission is "to help millions of people overseas and in the United States who suffer from hunger, poverty, and disease or from the ravages of war, oppression, and natural disasters." The ISA is made up of 55 diverse member agencies ranging from African medical relief funds to the Boy Scouts (overseas) and Catholic Charities. Information about each is provided. Contact ISA by phone at

(703) 548-2200, or toll free at (800) 638-8079 (United States only); fax: (703) 548-7685; e-mail: isa@dgs.dgsys.com. The street address is 66 Canal Center Plaza, Suite 310, Alexandria, VA 22314.

Internet Non-Profit Center: Home to Donors and Volunteers

http://www.human.com:80/inc/

The Internet Non-Profit Center has no paid staff. Initially sponsored by the American Institute of Philanthropy in 1994, the Center is now run by Cliff Landesman, who is solely responsible for the content of its publications, lists, and links to nonprofits. The Center does *not* list jobs, but it does provide documents describing hundreds of voluntary and nonprofit organizations, including financial data about organizations. Send e-mail to Cliff Landesman at clandesm@panix.com.

The National Civic League

http://www.csn.net/ncl

Founded in 1894 by Theodore Roosevelt, Louis Brandeis, and other turn-of-the-century progressives, the National Civic League (NCL) is a community-focused advocacy organization. The site highlights grassroots efforts from around the United States and covers every field, from prenatal care to parent education, from job training to school-based health clinics, from affordable housing to community-oriented policing. Contact by phone at (303) 571-4343 or by fax at (303) 571-4404.

soc.org.nonprofit

This newsgroup covers all topics related to nonprofits: funding, technology, programming, and so forth. It is one of the primary Internet resources for nonprofit administrators.

USNONPROFIT-L

To subscribe: majordomo@coyote.rain.org;

Message: subscribe usnonprofit-1

This Internet mailing list discusses nonprofit U.S. organizations. It is a mirror of the soc.org.nonprofit newsgroup, and, despite the title, has an international membership.

Social Sciences

Archaeology

Archaeological Fieldwork Server

http://durendal.cit.cornell.edu/

Individuals seeking archaeology field work opportunities can browse through postings, including positions for volunteers, full-time jobs, positions in field schools, contract jobs, and other archaeological postings that are submitted or found on mailing lists and in newsgroups. This service does not contain position announcements for professional academic and staff archaeologists. Positions are categorized by geographic location of the site or school. Contact Ken Stuart via e-mail at kps1@cornell.edu.

Career Counseling

JOBPLACE

listserv@news.jobweb.org

The National Association of Colleges and Employers (NACE) provides this mailing list as a network for professionals interested in discussing career development and employment strategies. Job announcements for career services professionals are included. The association maintains archives of postings on the JobWeb at http://www.jobweb.org.

JobWire

http://www.jobweb.org/jobwire.htm

Jobs for college career services and human resource professionals from *The Spotlight*, NACE's biweekly newsletter, are available from the most recent two issues. Contact the employers for more information and to apply for advertised listings.

Economics

JOE—Job Opportunities for Economists

gopher://vuinfo.vanderbilt.edu:70/11/employment/joe

The electronic version of Job Opportunities for Economists (JOE) is published as a service of Vanderbilt University. These are job listings reported by the members of the American Economic Association. Only the current month's file is available. The listings are arranged alphabetically by institution (note that "University of" is ignored in this arrangement), with U.S. academic positions first. This file is huge, so be prepared to wait while it loads.

Education and Evaluation

AIR-L, Electronic Newsletter of the Association for Institutional Research

To subscribe: listserv@vtvm1.cc.vt.edu

Message: subscribe AIR-L yourfirstname yourlastname

This newsletter has its own set of position announcements posted on the listserv. Contact Larry Nelson at NELSON_L@salt.plu.edu.

ERIC Clearinghouse on Research, Evaluation, and Measurement

http://www.cua.edu/www/eric_ae/

gopher://vmsgopher.cua.edu/11gopher_root_eric_ae%3a%5b_jobs%5d

The ERIC Clearinghouse lists jobs in the areas of research, statistics, assessment, evaluation, and learning theory. It also provides links to similar job resources elsewhere on the Internet.

University of Minnesota's College of Education Job Search Bulletin Board

gopher://rodent.cis.umn.edu:11119/

Listings for education and teaching jobs all over the United States in positions from elementary through college-level instruction are updated weekly, and the location of each job is included in the menu. The database is searchable by keyword. Fantastic resource!

English as a Second Language

TESLJB-L

To subscribe: listserv@cunyvm.cuny.edu.

message: subscribe TESLJB-L yourfirstname yourlastname

The Jobs and Employment issues sublist of TESL-L is at the same listserv address. *Note:* **Participants must be members of the TESL-L main list to join this list**, which discusses and announces job opportunities in the field of teaching English as a second language. For more information, contact Anthea Tillyer at ABTHC@cunyvm.cuny.edu.

*Law**

The Seamless Webs Legal Job Center

http://www.seamless.com/jobs/

The Seamless Web is a great resource for those in the law profession. On the job page, you can post an opportunity or a "position wanted" announcement at no cost. (You will have to sort the list since both types of announcements are interfiled.) Only job listings that directly relate to the legal profession will be posted. This is defined as those messages that seek or offer employment for lawyers, barristers, solicitors, legal assistants, paralegals, legal secretaries, and so on. Freelance legal or computer consultants, and/or law-related consulting companies are encouraged to contact the owners for information on their standard rates for promoting services.

* See also listings for the U.S. Department of Justice in Chapter 9.

*Library and Information Sciences**

ACRLNY-L

To subscribe: mailserv@acfcluster.nyu.edu

Message: subscribe acrlny-1 yourfirstname yourlastname

This Internet mailing list features library events and employment in New York. The list archives are available at ftp://acfcluster.nyu.edu. For more information, contact the moderator, Sue Schub, via e-mail at schub@acfcluster.nyu.edu.

BUBL Employment Bulletin Board

gopher://ukoln.bath.ac.uk:7070/11/Academic/Employment

This site includes extensive information resources for librarians and international employment opportunities for librarians in Britain, Europe, and the United States. For more information, contact Dennis Nicholson, Coordinating Editor, Strathclyde University Library, Glasgow, Scotland; e-mail: cijs03@vaxa.strath.ac.uk; phone: (0141)-552 3701, ext. 4632.

College and Research Libraries Jobs

gopher://gopher.uic.edu/11/library/crl/crljobs

These are primarily the academic job listings from the monthly *C&RL News*, published by the Association of College and Research Libraries, a division of the American Library Association. The listings are updated monthly and are available two to three weeks before the print version.

LIBJOB-L

Subscribe to: listserv@ubvm.cc.buffalo.edu

Message: subscribe libjob-1 yourfirstname yourlastname

This mailing list at SUNY Buffalo features entry-level library positions in New York state. For more information, contact Evan Morton via e-mail at v564s4g9@ubvms.cc.buffalo.edu.

Library Jobs and Employment: A Guide to Internet Resources by Jeff Lee

http://www.wpi.edu/Academics/IMS/Library/jobguide/libjobs.txt

gopher://una.hh.lib.umich.edu/00/inetdirsstacks/libjobs%3alee

In a professional paper compiled to fulfill the degree requirements for his MLS, Jeff has created a new listing of Internet resources to assist librarians with their online job searches. Information on searching the Internet and basic guides to Telnet, news, and so on are included.

* See also listings for ALIX and Library of Congress in Chapter 9.

Library Jobs and Library Employment: Navigating the Electronic Web by John Fenner

gopher://una.hh.lib.umich.edu/00/inetdirsstacks/jobs%3afenner

This was the first guide to help librarians with their search for employment. This is not being updated (date is January 1994), but it is very comprehensive.

LIS-JOBLIST

To subscribe: mailserv@ac.dal.ca

Message: subscribe LIS-JOBLIST

Lori Small at Dalhousie University is the moderator of this Internet mailing list discussing entry-level jobs in library and information studies. All postings are announcements for such positions within Atlantic Canada. Contact Lori for more information at lsmall@ac.dal.ca.

SLAJOB

To subscribe: listserv@iubvm.ucs.indiana.edu

Message: subscribe SLAJOB yourfirstname yourlastname

The Special Libraries Association mailing list discusses international opportunities for librarians. Contact Spencer Anspach (SANSPACH@ucs.indiana.edu) or Roger Beckman (BECKMANR @ucs.indiana.edu) for more information.

Southern Connecticut State University Library

http://www.scsu-cs.ctstateu.edu/library/careerpage.html

A must for librarians seeking jobs! Southern Connecticut State University provides links to its own Library Jobline, Lee's Library Jobs and Employment, *The Chronicle of Higher Education*, and numerous other great resources.

Univ. of Illinois, GSLIS Placement Online—Library Job Service

http://alexia.lis.uiuc.edu/gslis/research/jobsearch.html

telnet carousel.lis.uiuc.edu

login: jobs

Library positions nationwide are listed with the University of Illinois GSLIS. You can enter the database through the Web server, but you still use Telnet to connect and will need to register with your last name.

University of Texas Graduate School of Library and Information Science

http://fiat.gslis.utexas.edu/#placement

gopher://volvo.gslis.utexas.edu/11/placement/

This University of Texas server has links to a Gopher (gopher://volvo.gslis.utexas.edu) listing a dozen or so posted librarian jobs, and links to job resource documents and other online employment resources for librarians. Contact by phone at (512) 471-3821; fax: (512)-471-3971; or e-mail: www@gslis.utexas.edu.

Public Administration

Florida State Career Center Job Openings and Placement Help

http://www.fsu.edu/~spap/job/job.html

The Askew School of Public Administration and Policy at Florida State University maintains this server, which stresses job openings and related services for government employees and students in Florida State's Masters of Public Administration Program. Several lists of job links are standard and others lead to entry-level jobs. One unique link is a job bank titled "Academic Jobs from the American Association of Public Policy Analysis and Management" (http://www.fsu.edu:80/~spap/job/job.html). Send e-mail to David Coursey at spap@mailer.fsu.edu.

Psychology

American Psychological Society (APS) Observer Job Listings

http://www.hanover.edu/psych/APS/aps.html

gopher://gopher.hanover.edu:70/11/Hanover_College_Information/Psychology/APS/

The APS site has job listings in the social sciences and psychology, primarily college and university postings. It also includes job listings from the APS, news about the organization, and related psychology resources. Contact John H. Krantz, Ph.D., via e-mail at krantzj@hanover.edu.

Women's Studies

Employment Opportunities in Women's Studies and Feminism

gopher://gopher.inform.umd.edu:70/11/EdRes/Topic/WomensStudies/Employment

This directory is part of the Women's Studies Database at inforM, the University of Maryland, College Park Campus' online information system. Job postings include the closing date on the menu so you can see how close a deadline is. To submit information to this directory, contact Kathy Burdette at burdette@info.umd.edu.

CHAPTER 9

Jobs with the Federal Government

The federal government is one of the largest employers in the United States and probably the most diversified. You can find listings for employment opportunities in several locations online and can examine all of them at no charge, but you will have to register for the Telnet sites. *Be sure to check the dates on the listings and to note all job code numbers*. You may need specific forms in order to apply or you might be asked to include information with your application that is not on your résumé, so check for "**Information on Applying**" at any of the sites. **The Library of Congress** (**Chapter 3**) is a great place to start searching for information on the many federal departments and agencies.

Job Search Tip: Be enthusiastic about the position and about yourself! If you are not, the message will come out loud and clear every time you communicate with an employer (through cover letters and résumés, in phone and interview conversations). After all, why should someone hire you if you are not confident and positive about the job and what you can bring to it?
Judy A. Carbone, *Career Consultant, Career Development Center, George Mason University, Fairfax, VA.*

General Resources

FedWorld: The U.S. Government Bulletin Board

http://www.fedworld.gov/jobs.htm

telnet fedworld.doc.gov

ftp: //fwux.fedworld.gov/pub/jobs

Introduced by the National Technical Information Service (NTIS) in November 1992, FedWorld offers access to detailed information from over 50 government agencies. It also includes access to online ordering services, federal job opportunities, and dial-up access to other government information systems. To see the job opportunities listed with the U.S. Office of Personnel Management (OPM), select item **[J] Federal Job Openings** from the main menu. These job announcements can be searched by region or state, or they can be downloaded. Keep in mind that some of the files are quite large. Several agencies list their own job openings, so look for these within the agencies' separate menus.

Federal Job Opportunity Board (FJOB)

telnet fjob.mail.opm.gov

The Federal Job Opportunity Board is the official database of jobs listed with the Office of Personnel Management. All users must register with their name and location and choose a password. Some limited searches are available here which are not available on FedWorld. Applications are not accepted here, so if you see a job that interests you, contact the agency that posted it for more information. Report any connection problems to (912) 757-3030.

Federal Jobs Database from NACE

http://www.jobweb.org/fedjobsr.htm

This database of federal jobs is keyword searchable, and you can select the state(s) you wish to search. Both form and process are very simple. Information on applying for federal jobs is available along with the standard form which can be used in lieu of your résumé. There is specific information that must be included and may not be part of your traditional résumé, so be sure to read this document carefully before applying for any positions.

Federal Information Exchange, Inc. (FEDIX)

http://web.fie.com/

gopher://gopher.fie/com:70/

telnet fedix.fie.com

An alternative site to FedWorld, FEDIX provides information about approximately ten federal agencies, including employment opportunities for some. Not a complete listing, but it does offer a choice of listings by agency. For more information, send e-mail to webmaster@fedix.fie.com.

FinanceNet

http://www.financenet.gov/

Fin-jobs

To subscribe: listproc@financenet.gov

message: SUBSCRIBE fin-jobs yourname

fnet.fin.jobs (usenet newsgroup)

news-fin-jobs@financenet.gov

FinanceNet encourages discussion among and provides information for individuals in the public finance sector. Its main menu links to related resources, OPM's Federal Job Bank, information about state and local government and their professional organizations, and information about FinanceNet-sponsored discussion forums and mailing lists. Federal, state, and local government agencies are encouraged to post their appropriate vacancies to the **fin-jobs mailing list** and its corresponding discussion group. The corresponding Usenet newsgroup, which can also be posted to via e-mail, has been developed to encourage a dialogue on issues relating to employment in the public financial management professions. For more information or assistance, send e-mail to fin-jobs@financenet.gov or support@financenet.gov.

FedJobs, The Federal Job Bulletin Board

ftp://listserv-ftp.dartmouth.edu/pub/listserv/fedjobs/

To subscribe: listserv@dartmouth.edu

Message: SUB FEDJOBS Yourfirstname yourlastname

FedJobs provides access to job announcements posted by the Office of Personnel Management, which acts as the personnel office and recruitment agency for the federal government. It also houses a wealth of information files for job searching with the federal government and other resources. The e-mail subscription will add your name to the list of people who are notified when new files are added to the server. You will *not* be sent any of the files, which can be enormous. This service is a project of David Avery of Dartmouth College and David Valley of the Department of Labor, and is not supported by the federal government. It is provided to make it easier to retrieve the job listings, and Dartmouth College and the two maintainers do not accept responsibility for the accuracy or format of the information. For more information, contact the list owner, David Avery, via e-mail at David.Avery@dartmouth.edu.

CAPACCESS, National Capital Area Public Access Network

telnet capaccess.org

login: guest, **password:** visitor

Job listings are given here for the Washington, DC area, including some government openings. At the prompt, type **go career**.

Specific Departments and Agencies

dod.jobs

This is a newsgroup for posting job announcements from the U.S. Department of Defense.

ALIX, Automated Library Information Xchange

telnet alix.loc.gov 3001

login with your first and last name

A service of the Federal Library and Information Center Committee, Federal Library Network, ALIX features both federal and nonfederal library positions. Select **[B]ulletin** from the menu to see the job listings.

Library of Congress

gopher://marvel.loc.gov/11/employee/employ

The Library of Congress lists its own employment opportunities and provides additional pointers to other job listings online. Not everything here is for librarians!

U.S. Department of Justice

gopher://justice2.usdoj.gov/1/jobs (*Job listings for Attorneys.*)

gopher://justice2.usdoj.gov:70/11/careers (*Postings for all other positions.*)

The jobs listed with the Justice Department are primarily for attorneys, but a separate listing for nonattorney positions is also available.

National Science Foundation

gopher://x.nsf.gov/11/NSF/vacancies

Job listings for the National Science Foundation (NSF) include some old job positions, so be sure to check the dates on any announcements you are interested in. The NSF Web server does not include this information.

Department of the Interior Automated Vacancy Announcement Distribution System (AVADS)

http: //www.usgs.gov/doi/avads/index.html

Announcements for jobs with the many branches of the Department of the Interior, including the Park Service, Indian Affairs, Land Management, and the Geological Survey, are found here. AVADS can also be accessed through **FedJobs** (described earlier).

U.S. Fish & Wildlife Service

http://www.fws.gov/employmt.html

The Fish & Wildlife Service (FWS) homepage provides a great deal of information about the service's functions and ongoing projects, and careers in FWS. It also links to the **AVADS** listing of Department of the Interior jobs, which includes positions at the FWS.

CHAPTER 10

State and Local Opportunities for Employment

The resources in this chapter are specific to a city, state, or region of the United States and include several Usenet newsgroups, freenets (local community networks), regional services, and state governments with online information services. We did not include the hundreds of U.S. colleges and universities in this list, but you can easily find them by using The **WWW Master List of Web Servers** and The **Mother Gopher** noted in the resource list in **Chapter 4**. These institutions usually collect information pertinent to their local communities and list their own employment opportunities on their public servers.

Community freenets frequently carry local job listings and might also provide all kinds of information for a region, including available housing and lists of local businesses. Although each freenet is organized differently, you can generally find helpful career information in the listings of government resources and services, community centers, and libraries. Business or commercial resources may give the names of companies or people to contact about potential work opportunities. The downside of the freenets is that many restrict access to good information to registered members only. If this is so, see if you can register as a user.

The number of local resources for employment opportunities and information is growing tremendously, particularly with state governments coming online. Many states are putting their own employment opportunities online as well as offering connections to Job Service opportunities for employment all over the state. Since each state has a slightly different arrangement of responsibilities for its agencies, look for departments or agencies with "Personnel," "Human Resources," "Labor," or "Employment" in their titles. A project is underway at this time to bring the job databases of all 50 state employment service agencies onto the Internet through America's Job Bank in cooperation with the U.S. Department of Labor.

If a state did not have its job listings online at the time of this writing, it was not included here. That does not mean the missing states do not have these services available now. If your state employment service agency doesn't appear in our list, check to see if it's mentioned at either of these sites.

State and Local Government on the Net
http://www.piperinfo.com/piper/state/states.html

Library of Congress Information on State and Local Governments
http://lcweb.loc.gov/global/state/stategov.html

Our listing of state government resources was researched through the first list, which is compiled by Dana Noonan, a computing and Internet consultant in Minnesota. He continually updates this list as new services are announced by the states and various local governments, so check with him for the latest information. You can contact Dana for more information on this project at **piper@webcom.com** or **noonan@msus1.msus.edu**. The Library of Congress has linked together several similar lists and other resources that can lead you to good information about a region.

State and local government servers can be fantastic sources of information! They not only present their own information, they present lists of businesses within the state, educational institutions, and other leads to help you out. The state employment services have incredible lists of opportunities waiting for you to walk in the door and view, or surf into their site and browse. **You support these with your tax dollars, so use them!**

America's Job Bank is adding links to individual state employment security agencies as they come online. At the time of this writing, 14 separate states were on the Internet with their job databanks, and the number is increasing monthly. Check the individual states through Dana's list, or use **America's Job Bank** to jump directly to the list of these agencies through their site: **http: //www.ajb.dni.us/**

> **Job Search Tip:** Skills are the bait of a job search. Without good ones, well presented, you are fishing with an empty hook.
> **Dr. William Stowe**, *Associate Director of Career Services, Texas Christian University*

States are presented in alphabetical order with state government services listed first. All other resources within the state are listed alphabetically by name after that.

Alabama

hsv.jobs

This is a newsgroup for jobs in Huntsville, AL.

Alaska

Anchorage Daily News

http://www.adn.com/

The *Daily News* is adding the classified ads to their server. Links to several resources in Alaska are also included, making this a nice starting point for the state.

Arizona

az.jobs

This is a newsgroup for jobs in Arizona.

Arkansas

uark.jobs

This newsgroup lists jobs at the University of Arkansas.

California

California State Government

http://www.ca.gov/

ftp://ftp.teale.ca.gov/pub

California was a leader in bringing state information online, and it shows. Excellent representation of their state with legislative information, agencies, and other resources are all linked together. Use this main site to access it all!

Living, Learning & Working in California

http://agency.resource.ca.gov/gov/living.html

A part of the official state Web server, this ties together state programs, agencies, opportunities for employment and education, and information about living in California. It has great information presented so it's easy to use.

ba.jobs.contract

This newsgroup is for contract jobs around the San Francisco Bay Area.

ba.jobs.misc

This newsgroup discusses jobs and job hunting in the San Francisco Bay Area.

ba.jobs.offered

This newsgroup features jobs around the San Francisco Bay Area.

ba.jobs.resumes

This newsgroup provides a place for résumés of job seekers in the San Francisco Area.

24-Hours, Recorded Job Lines for the San Francisco Bay Area

http://www.webcom.com/~rmd/bay_area/joblines.html

An excellent starting point for a Bay Area job search, this site lists jobline numbers for the Bay Area, as well as pointers to other local employment resources and online job listings. For more information, contact Gina di Gualco via e-mail at regina@netcom.com.

California Career and Employment Center

http://www.webcom.com/~career/

A division of Help Wanted USA, this is one of the largest online recruiters around. This site concentrates on positions in California and links to some interesting career services and information. Information on employers who are members is available, as are links to the Online Career Center and other regional Help Wanted USA offices. Other information resources are planned.

Chancellor & Chancellor

http://www.chancellor.com

Chancellor & Chancellor, based in Marin County, CA, is a broker for contract and full-time software engineers in the Silicon Valley. The company's Web site contains available contracts and permanent positions, along with information about its 401K and health plan benefits and a photo gallery of the staff. Address questions to andre@chancellor.com.

Coolware

http://www.coolware.com/jobs/jobs.html

Updated each day, this database of jobs, mainly for the San Francisco Bay Area, has positions submitted locally as well as copied from other sources. Coolware has lots of great listings that can be searched by keyword or browsed by broad topics. Also in the works is a Bay Locator map to let you click on a section of a map and pull up all of job listings within that area. Contact kcooley@none.coolware.com with any questions.

la.jobs

This newsgroup is for jobs in or around Los Angeles.

MindSource Software

http://www.mindsrc.com/reqs.html

MindSource is a family-owned-and-operated consulting company for independent contractors that specializes in Unix System and

Network administration, and World Wide Web administration and development. All current positions are located in the San Francisco Bay Area.

Palo Alto Weekly

http://www.service.com/PAW/home.html

This is a local newspaper from Palo Alto, CA. Check the classifieds for employment opportunities, and, if you miss a day, you can also check the back issues. It includes lots of great listings and apartment information should you need it.

San Francisco Bay Area Web Guide

http://www.hyperion.com/ba/sfbay.html

Advertisements from individual companies and collections of classifieds from area newspapers are well indexed. A wealth of community/relocation information is available. *This is an awesome site!* Contact Steven Grimn at koreth@hyperion.com for more information.

San Francisco Chronicle and Examiner

http://www.sfgate.com/

San Francisco's daily newspapers include online links to the help wanted ads. The URL **http://sfgate.com/classifieds/index.html** goes directly to the classified section. Look through other sections of the newspaper for housing information or to find out more about the Bay area. There is a keyword-searchable, separate classifieds section from the most recent Sunday paper. Unfortunately, you could wade through pages before getting to the job opportunities. Use the "Find" command in your browser to locate "job opportunities" and get around that problem.

San Jose Mercury

http://www.sjmercury.com/class/help/index.htm

This particular link takes you directly to the San Jose, CA, newspaper's "Help Wanted" ads. You can search today's ads or the ads from the past Sunday edition, or browse by broad categories. You might want to read other areas of the newspaper for more information and connections to additional Bay Area links.

San Mateo Times

http://www.baynet.com/smtimes/market/classified/index.html

This URL takes you to the classified ad index for the San Mateo–area newspaper. Follow the links to a short list of local employment agencies, "Employment Wanted," or "Help Wanted."

sdnet.jobs

This newsgroup is for jobs around San Diego County, CA.

slac.jobs

This newsgroup lists jobs at the Stanford Linear Accelerator Center, Stanford, CA.

The SofTech Jobs Board

http://sbt.sbtcorp.com:80/~softech/stjobs.html

The North Bay Software and Information Technology Association in Marin County is a nonprofit organization dedicated to the advancement of software and information technology. SofTech's mission is to foster communication and cooperation among North Bay software and information technology companies with the goal of strengthening local industry and increasing the region's economic prosperity. Select the companies listed to view their available job openings.

su.jobs

This newsgroup lists jobs at Stanford University.

Trinity Partners

http://www.trinity1.com/welcome.html

This contract consulting firm for computing and data processing personnel in California offers listings for both permanent and contract placement, and résumés can be submitted to the résumé database. Additional links to Internet job resources will take you to some other services covered in this book along with other recruiting agencies.

ucb.jobs

This newsgroup presents jobs at or around University of California, Berkeley.

ucd.cs.jobs

This newsgroup is for computer science jobs at or around University of California, Davis.

ucd.kiosk.jobs

This is a newsgroup listing general jobs at or around University of California, Davis.

Webdog's Job Hunt

http://itec.sfsu.edu/jobs.html

This great up-to-date site of general and San Francisco Bay area resources provides links to job listings, as well as the classified sections of area newspapers. Contact Jeff Schwartz at webdog@ sfsu.edu for more information.

Job Search Tip: If you are relocating, monitor the Usenet newsgroups for the area you are moving to for job listings and other good information about the area.

Colorado

State of Colorado

http://www.state.co.us/

The State Department of Employment and Labor includes employment statistics and other resources, in addition to the job services it provides for both employers and job seekers. Links to many community networks and information services are included.

Boulder Community Network

http://bcn.boulder.co.us/

The Boulder Community Network connects you to the city of Boulder along with county information and job listings, and several other Colorado-specific job resources. The Employment Center is a wonderful collection of information and links to employment opportunities in the Boulder area and throughout the state.

Connecticut

Jobline, School of Library Science and Instructional Technology

http://www.scsu-cs.ctstateu.edu/library/jobline.html

Jobs in libraries in Connecticut and the Northeast are listed here. Not all of these jobs are for professional librarians, but they are all in or related to libraries. The Connecticut jobs are listed first, and the newsletter is published twice a month during the academic year. It is a service of the library school at Southern Connecticut State University.

ne.jobs

ne.jobs.contract

Both of these newsgroups are for jobs in New England.

Delaware

Index of Delaware Web Sites from Delaware Technical and Community College

http://www.dtcc.edu/delaware/

Employment opportunities in Delaware are collected and link both local organizations and companies, and resources from other locations (Online Career Center, and so on). Either click on "Businesses" and then page down to "Employment" or use the "find" feature in your browser to get to "Employment" more quickly.

District of Columbia

balt.jobs

This is a newsgroup for jobs in the Baltimore/Washington, DC area.

dc.jobs

This newsgroup lists jobs in Washington, DC, and surrounding areas.

CAPACCESS, National Capitol Area Public Access Network

telnet capaccess.org

login: guest, password: visitor

At the prompt, type "go career" (no quotes).

http://www.capaccess.org

This network provides job listings for the Washington, DC, area, including some government openings and a list of local employment agencies. You might also want to explore other menus, such as the "Business and Professional" section for more career and community information. The Web server is intended to supplement the Telnet database, not replace it.

Florida

Florida Communities Network (FCN)

http://www.state.fl.us/

gopher://gopher.state.fl.us/

This is the major link to Florida information. Browse through this site by category for best access. It is graphic intensive, but provides a link for text-only viewing.

Access Government Job Opportunities In Florida

http://www.state.fl.us/fcn/centers/job_center/vacany/

This is a fantastic service! Updated weekly, this link to the FCN includes job listings for government agencies all over the state. You can search regions or the entire state at once, then narrow your search by occupation. The resulting list gives you a job title and full description, a pay grade, a phone number for contact, and the opportunity to apply online.

fl.jobs

This is a newsgroup for jobs in Florida.

fsu.jobs

This newsgroup provides announcements for jobs at or near Florida State University (FSU).

Job Board, Florida State University

http://www.fsu.edu/Jobs.html

Job Board, located at Florida State University, includes job postings for all the state universities in Florida. Position listings include faculty, administration, and support personnel. Information on salary ranges can be found here as well. There are links to other internal resources (such as job listings in computer science provided by that department at FSU) and additional links to external academic position resources.

Tallahassee Free-net

http://www.freenet.scri.fsu.edu/

http://freenet3.scri.fsu.edu:81/

telnet freenet3.scri.fsu.edu
login:visitor

Tallahassee has created a very nice information network. Select "Business and Professions" to connect to the employment opportunities. The job-listing services are divided into "Florida" and "WorldWide." All worldwide resources are unavailable to visitors via Telnet as are many of the Florida resources. Some sites are open to visitors and carry great listings.

Georgia

State of Georgia

http://www.state.ga.us/

gopher://gopher.doas.state.ga.us/

Job listings for the state are under the "Merit System of Personnel Administration Job Information" section of the state's homepage. There are two categories of job listings, constant recruitment and time sensitive. You might check both lists to see if they have a specific opening or if they are always on the lookout for employees in your field. Also included is an excellent file of preliminary information on how to apply for these jobs and other helpful resources. At the time of this writing, the Web site linked back to the Gopher for the job information.

alt.jobs

This newsgroup covers positions available in Atlanta.

Atlanta CyberJobs

http://www.cy.com/jobs/

Atlanta CyberJobs has openings in and around Atlanta. There is no charge to add a job listing to the site. Current categories include administration, management, data processing, sales, and miscellaneous jobs, which had some nanny and sales clerk openings when reviewed. An interesting little feature is a map of Atlanta and the surrounding region to show you where the jobs are located.

Atlanta Web Guide

http://www.webguide.com/

With a virtual tour as its centerpiece, the Atlanta Web Guide is the closest you can come to visiting a city without paying the airfare! It is an excellent model for other cities to emulate. Sunbelt Advertising maintains this site featuring local companies' products, restaurants, and interesting sites for tourists to visit. It links to universities in the area that provide an entree to job sites, if you're willing to work through half a dozen layers. Contact the guide by phone at (404) 847-0181; fax: (404) 257-1047; or e-mail: webguide@webguide.com.

Atlanta's Computer Job Store

http://www.ComputerJobs.com/

Industry and career information for computer professionals in the Atlanta area is provided here. There is great information on the Atlanta job market for computer professionals, job listings, information on the companies in the Atlanta area (not just those who advertise here), and a skill registry. Great-looking site.

git.ohr.jobs.digest

This is a newsgroup for listings provided by the Georgia Institute of Technology.

Hawaii

The Maui News

http://www.maui.net/~mauinews/news.html

This site includes the help wanted ads from the daily newspaper. They are buried inside of other sections, so you will need to scroll down the page.

Idaho

Idaho Department of Employment

http://www.doe.state.id.us/

Idaho labor information, job search and job training programs, and other information to assist both the employer and the job seeker are given here. As with other similar services, you can do a self-directed search or use the Dictionary of Occupational Titles (DOT) code numbers for searching. Very simple forms lead you to select occupational field, location, and the position announcements you want to view. To apply, print the page with the job description or jot down the job number and DOT code and contact any Idaho Job Service office. The list of these offices is on the server and available from each job page. From the main state homepage at **http://www.state.id.us/**, choose "Topical Index" and the letter "E" to access the employment services page.

Internet Tip: Your **Web browser** can be used to read news through the World Wide Web. Two things must be set up at *your* site to let this work: Your Web browser must be *configured*, or set up, to read news, and your local provider must carry the newsgroups you want to read. If a problem occurs, talk to your own help desk before you send messages.

Illinois

chi.job

This is a newsgroup for jobs in Chicago.

Chicago Mosaic

http://www.ci.chi.il.us

A service of the City of Chicago, National Center for Supercomputing Applications, and University of Illinois (Urbana-Champaign and Chicago campuses), this doesn't give you job listings, but it does give you a contact name and phone number for the personnel department.

Chicago Tribune

http://www.chicago.tribune.com/

One of the major newspapers for Chicago, the *Tribune* posts the help wanted sections from the past three Sundays online. You are better off with a graphical browser for the more powerful search features, but Lynx users can browse the listings. Check out the "Feature" articles for job tips, and the "Profiles of Local Companies" to get information about Chicago businesses. Very nicely done.

Heartland Regional Network, the Community Network for Central Illinois

telnet heartland.bradley.edu

login: bbguest, **password:** *press* RETURN

Heartland includes a link to the Illinois Department of Employment Security (IDES) and sample job listings from that agency. Choose "Government Center" from the main menu, then "State Government" and "IDES." These listings include the job title, description, and pay rate. To apply for a job, you must contact IDES.

il.jobs.misc

This newsgroup is available for discussions about work in Illinois.

il.jobs.offered

This newsgroup lists jobs available in Illinois.

il.jobs.resumes

This newsgroup is for résumé postings by persons in or seeking employment in Illinois.

uiuc.cs.jobs

This newsgroup lists computer science jobs at the University of Illinois.

uiuc.misc.jobs

This is a newsgroup for general job announcements at the University of Illinois, Urbana-Champaign.

Indiana

State Government Job Bank

http://www.state.in.us/acin/personnel/index.html

The Department of Personnel provides this searchable job bank on the Internet. You can opt to view it in its entirety (not recommended), you can download it (only if you must), or you can search the Job Bank in some unique ways. Begin by choosing to search by city, job title, or job family (professional, clerical, and so on). You will be taken through menus to narrow your search until the results are presented. Information on applying for positions is available along with a guide to the cryptic abbreviations used in the listings.

in.jobs

This newsgroup lists jobs in Indiana.

Iowa

Iowa Jobs Information from the Department of Employment Services (DES)

http://www.state.ia.us/jobs/index.html

Iowa has linked together full-time and part-time job listings, jobs available with the state, and information on finding federal job listings. Job openings are sorted by the city in which they are located, so use the "find" feature in your Web browser to locate keywords. This information can also be accessed via dial-up modem at (800) 572-3472 in Iowa or (515) 281-3472 from out of state. The list of Iowa Job Workforce offices is available on the DES homepage at http://www.state.ia.us/government/des/.

Kansas

Information Network of Kansas

http://www.ink.org

telnet ink.org

login: inkguest.

The Kansas Department of Human Resources provides access to ALEX for visitors and registered users alike, Monday through Friday from 6:30 A.M. to 6:30 P.M. central standard time. ALEX is the Automated Labor EXchange, a nationwide database of jobs listed with the various state job services. It can take a minute or two to connect, and it operates slowly, but it can be beneficial. *Take notice of the exit command for the system!* A separate "Federal Opportunities" search has 58 categories to choose from. The menus are similar to America's Job Bank, but a duplicate search in that database did not reveal the same job listings. *Search both!*

Kentucky

No resources are currently available.

Louisiana

Department of Labor (DOL)

http://www.ldol.state.la.us/

One of the finest Web services available for users, the DOL server includes a set of frequently asked questions (FAQs) for employers, job seekers, and others who need its services, as well as links to exceptional job and career information. The Job Information Service (JIS) allows you to search the state by geographic location and then job family (professional, clerical, and so on). Note: Teaching and education jobs have been separated into a different database. The DOL has provided an excellent service for all users, but includes some particularly helpful articles and links for entry-level job seekers and new high school and college graduates. You can easily reach this from the main page of the **Info Louisiana** server at **http://www.state.la.us/** by just clicking on "job listings."

lou.lft.jobs

This newsgroup covers jobs in Lafayette.

Maine

Maine State Government

http://www.state.me.us/

Maine has built a very nice Web server for the state government, including a link to current state job openings divided into three sections. "Current Jobs" is a list of specific jobs the state is hiring for, while the "Continuous Recruitment" section lists job titles for which the state always accepts applications. The "Direct Hire" agencies are listed in this job information page with their addresses and phone numbers. Because these agencies have very specific needs for personnel, they do their own hiring. Job applications are accepted online, but check for information on proper application procedures. Some positions may require special forms.

ne.jobs

ne.jobs.contract

These newsgroups are for jobs in New England.

Maryland

Department of Library Services: Sailor

gopher://sailor.lib.md.us/

Sailor will connect you to both state and community information. Use the "Find information by topic" link to get general job information, then select "Government Information" to find the information for the various state agencies in Maryland. The Enoch Pratt Free Library, the State Office of Personnel, and the University of Maryland at College Park all have job listings available through this service. State listings are updated weekly.

balt.jobs

This newsgroup lists jobs in the Baltimore/Washington, DC, area.

Massachusetts

Massachusetts Internet Job Bank, Department of Employment and Training (DET)

http://ma.jobsearch.org

Employment opportunities in or near Massachusetts with contacts for all local DET offices are provided here. If you are not in Massachusetts, you may fax or mail your résumé to an office. When forwarding your résumé, you must cite the job order number for which you are applying and your Social Security number.

If employer information is given in a listing, you may contact the employer directly. This site can be accessed through the **MAGNet** server for the Massachusetts government at **http:/www.magnet.state.ma.us/**.

City of Cambridge Employment Opportunities

http://www.ci.cambridge.ma.us/employment.html

Cambridge, just across the river from Boston and home to MIT and Harvard, has job listings and employment information for the city, the youth services program, and links to more information on this server. It also provides a resource called "High-Tech in Cambridge," which links together the high-tech companies in the Cambridge area. Many of these organizations post job opportunities on their servers.

Employment Opportunities in New England from Boston Online

http://www.std.com/NE/employment.html

A collection of links to help you find work in Boston and Massachusetts, Employment Opportunities includes links to the NYNEX yellow pages, SEC filings, and a list of Boston-area businesses. Only a few of the resources are duplicated in the Cambridge list already discussed.

MCET and MCET member job openings

http://meol.mass.edu:70/0/WWW/MCET/jobs.html

The Massachusetts Corporation for Educational Telecommunications (MCET) has job postings here for teaching and educational support positions in a variety of Massachusetts and New England schools. This server can be very slow, so be patient.

ne.jobs

ne.jobs.contract

These newsgroups are for jobs in New England.

Michigan

mi.jobs

This newsgroup covers jobs in Michigan.

mi.wanted

This is a newsgroup for jobs wanted in Michigan.

umich.jobs

This newsgroup lists jobs at the University of Michigan.

Minnesota

Minnesota Department of Economic Security

http://mn.jobsearch.org

The residents of this state have two powerful job search tools at their disposal, the Minnesota Job Search and the Minnesota SkillsNet. The Minnesota Job Search provides online access to its jobs database, labor market information, and unemployment information. You do have to negotiate past several pages to get to the job listings, but it is worth the effort. Once you have identified a job you'd like to apply for, fill out the online form, print it, and mail or fax the form with your résumé or statement of qualifications to the employment service office noted on the form. Phone inquiries are not accepted. The office will review your information and forward it to the employer, who will contact you directly. The Minnesota SkillsNet uses the latest technology to scan your résumé into its electronic database. Your education, experience, and up to 80 skills are identified and screened continuously against job openings listed with the job service. If your résumé is matched to an opening, you will be called before your résumé is sent to an employer. *What a service!*

METRONET

http://www.metronet.lib.mn.us:9003/

gopher://gopher.metronet.lib.mn.us:9003/

METRONET is a multitype library organization serving academic, public, and special libraries in the Twin Cities (Minneapolis-St. Paul). The server offers a searchable database of the METRONET list archive, the MetroLine BBS calendar, jobline, and freebies databases, and a selection of Internet guides and newsletters. It has a modest number of listings. Contact Mary Treacy, Director, via e-mail at mary.treacy@metronet.lib.mn.us or by regular mail at Metronet, 2324 University Ave. W., Suite 116, St. Paul, MN 55114; phone: (612) 646-0475; or fax: (612) 646-0657.

Twin Cities Free-Net

http://freenet.msp.mn.us/

telnet free-net.mpls-stpaul.mn.us

login: guest

Set up to serve the Minneapolis-St. Paul region, Twin Cities has a very nice selection of links to information and resources for the area. Select the "Resources by Subject" to find the business and employment section with its links to the Twin Cities jobs page and other great local resources, including the Minnesota Department of Employment Security Job Bank and several local businesses.

umn.cs.jobs

This newsgroup is for jobs at the University of Minnesota, Computer Science Department.

umn.general.jobs

This newsgroup is for general job postings from the University of Minnesota.

Mississippi

No resources are currently available.

Missouri

State of Missouri Merit System Job Opportunities

http://www.state.mo.us/oa/pers/jobopps.htm

You will find job opportunities with the State of Missouri listed here. Applications must be postmarked by midnight of the closing date stated in the announcement for each class. Only official applications may be filed, photocopies are not accepted. Official forms may be obtained from the Missouri Division of Personnel; or offices of the Divisions of Employment Security, Family Services, or Youth Services; or the Departments of Mental Health or Health and Corrections. For more information, contact the State of Missouri Office of Administration, Division of Personnel, Attn: Internet Coordinator, P.O. Box 388, Jefferson City, MO 65102; phone: (314) 751-4162; telecommunications device for the deaf (TDD): (314) 526-4488.

stl.jobs

This newsgroup is for jobs in or near St. Louis.

Montana

Montana Job Service

http://jsd_server.dli.mt.gov/

This server is full of information to help you find work in Montana, with links to additional Internet resources. You can do a self-directed search by occupational category and location. Each listing includes the job title and a brief description, pay rate, and location. After you find a position that interests you, you can view the list of Job Service offices within the region where you can apply for the job. State government jobs are included on this server within the "Other Places to Visit" section, and the listings are categorized by the recruiting agency. Job announcements are updated daily.

Nebraska

Nebraska Department of Personnel

http://www.state.ne.us/personnel/per.html

These weekly job listings for the state of Nebraska are divided by job type—part time, temporary, vocation/trade, professional, and so on. Listed first are the jobs still open from the previous week. New job listings include the position title, full description, job code, and pay rate. Some postings include notes about additional requirements or special application procedures. The contact address and phone number for the Nebraska Department of Personnel is at the bottom of the file. It refers to local job offices, but does not provide directory information online.

Omaha CareerLink

http://www.omaha.org/careerlink.html

Omaha CareerLink is maintained by the Applied Information Management (AIM) Institute in cooperation with The Greater Omaha Chamber of Commerce Labor Availability Council's Technical Committee. It matches professionals and college interns with available Nebraska job openings. Information on the companies is also provided. Well organized and user friendly. Contact Kandace Bragg, Employment Director via e-mail at kbragg@omaha.org or by phone at (402) 422-3194.

Nevada

The Sunday Paper

http://www.sundaypaper.com

This "online classified ad network and emporium" includes a section for classified ads (with a section for help wanted) which are not limited to the Las Vegas–Clark County region. However, if you go down to "Help Wanted by Locality," you will find the job openings for the Clark County Personnel Department. This list is updated weekly, and contact information for applying is at the top of the list. The "Net Travel Links" section includes some of the job resources covered in this book. Contact info@sundaypaper.com for more information.

New Hampshire

State of New Hampshire

http://www.state.nh.us/

This server, maintained by the New Hampshire State Library, is a growing resource for the state. At the time of review, the Employment Security Department did not have its job listings on the Internet, but information on connecting to the dial-up NH Works Bulletin Board is included for both in-state and out-of-state job seekers.

ne.jobs

ne.jobs.contract

Both of these newsgroup are for jobs in the New England area.

New Jersey

NJ JOBS

http://www.njjobs.com/

A service of Advanced Interactive Communications, Inc., NJ JOBS is an exclusive job opening service for New Jersey businesses.

Jobs are posted according to the week they are received, and they are listed alphabetically by job title. Use the "find" feature of your Web browser to look for keywords. Contact an employer directly to apply for a listed position. All questions should be forwarded to info@njjobs.com.

New Mexico

nm.jobs

This newsgroup covers jobs in New Mexico.

New York

Department of Labor

http://www.labor.state.ny.us/

Somewhat graphic intensive, but a welcome addition to the Internet, this site is similar in structure to other state banks with easy forms to guide you to job descriptions. If you want to apply for a job found on this database, fill out the online form, print it, and fax or mail it to the office indicated on the form. If you have not previously registered with the employment offices, include your résumé or statement of qualifications with the form. If you have already registered, merely print the form and send it in. The list of state employment service offices is included with the Community Service Offices online.

Employment Opportunities in New York City

http://www.panix.com/clay/nyc/employment.html

This service is maintained by Clay Irving as a part of the New York City Reference Page. The site, regularly updated to reflect available opportunities in the New York City area, provides a description for each listing so you can tell what you are connecting to. It also includes a link to the **Red Guide to Temp Agencies** (see listing in this section) with evaluations and information on the various temporary agencies in New York City.

Forum Personnel, Inc.

http://www.brainlink.com/~forum

New York–based employment search firm specializing in computer-related disciplines, such as programming, networking, technical support, multimedia, and Internet. Selected job listings are available online. Forum does a local business in and around New York City.

li.jobs

This newsgroup is for jobs in Long Island.

nyc.jobs.contract

This newsgroup covers contract positions in New York City.

nyc.jobs.misc

This newsgroup discusses job hunting in New York City.

nyc.jobs.offered

This is a newsgroup for jobs offered in New York City.

nyc.jobs.wanted

This is a newsgroup for jobs wanted in New York City.

The Red Guide to Temp Agencies

http://www.best.com/~ezy/redguide.html

Not just a guide to temporary agencies in New York, the Red Guide offers advice on how best to work the temp agencies. Agencies are evaluated for types of jobs staffed, pay rate, general length of employment, and other comments. These reviews are done by temps who have either had outstanding or awful experiences and want to pass the good or bad word on to you.

Syracuse Sunday Herald American

http://dataserver.syr.edu:8080/syrol/classifieds/jobs.html

These classified ads from the most current *Sunday Herald American* include jobs arranged by major categories as found in the newspaper (business, general, professional, and so on). The maintainers of this site suggest you use the "find" feature in your Web browser to locate the listings you are interested in by keyword.

North Carolina

North Carolina Employment Security Commission (NCESC)

http://www.esc.state.nc.us/

This is a wonderful service to use. The NCESC has created Internet Job Information Services (IJIS), a searchable database of all currently open positions listed with the state. There are two ways to access the job listings. If you choose the IJIS link, you are asked to select an occupational group, a job category, and then the region of the state you're interested in. If you opt for the IJIS Form, enter the job title you are interested in, a minimum pay rate, minimum education level, and minimum level of experience, and the form will return up to 25 matches for your request. All jobs are updated daily between 4 A.M. and 5 A.M. EST. This service is also accessible through the **State of North Carolina** main page at **http://www.sips.state.nc.us/.**

Office of State Personnel Job Vacancies

http://www.ncsu.edu/jobs/osp

These state government jobs are listed by major categories and can be read by job title or job location. Information on the applications is available in the "General Information" file, and some special forms may be required. This site can also be reached through the main server for the state at **http://www.sips.state.nc.us/.**

Forsyth County, Winston-Salem

http://www.co.forsyth.nc.us/JOBS/jobs.html

Jobs with the county, which includes Winston-Salem, are listed here. To apply, you must meet all minimum requirements and submit a complete application to the Personnel Office, Suite 709, Hall of Justice, Winston-Salem, NC 27101, on or before the closing date. To request an application form or for special assistance, please contact the Personnel office at (910) 727-2851 or e-mail to gearhace@athena.co.forsyth.nc.us.

The News and Observer Classifieds, Raleigh, North Carolina

gopher://merlin.nando.net/11/nando/classads

The online *News and Observer* is one of many services available at this site. The classified ads in this electronic newspaper cover the Raleigh/Durham/Chapel Hill area, otherwise known as the Research Triangle. You can check today's or tomorrow's ads, or the ads from the past Sunday.

The Nonprofit/Fundraising JobNet, Philanthropy Journal of North Carolina

http://www.nando.net/philant/philant.html

Interested in work as a development officer, nonprofit account manager, or director of planned giving? These jobs are concentrated in, but not exclusive to, the North Carolina area. The JobLink on the front page is the current month's listings, but each back issue has its JobLink area included.

North Dakota

No resources are currently available.

Ohio

Employment Opportunities, State of Ohio

gopher://gizmo.freenet.columbus.oh.us:70/11/governmentcenter/stateofohio

This is a summary of the jobs posted by the Centralized Recruitment and Referral Center for the State of Ohio. The list is updated weekly and includes a brief description of each position. The jobs are arranged alphabetically by agency and title. This site can be accessed through the State of Ohio homepage at **http://www.ohio.gov**. Select the link for "Other State Government Information."

cinci.jobs

This newsgroup covers jobs in Cincinnati.

cle.jobs

This newsgroup covers jobs in Cleveland.

cmh.jobs

This newsgroup covers jobs in Columbus.

Greater Columbus Freenet, Columbus OH

gopher://gizmo.freenet.columbus.oh.us

Guest access from outside Greater Columbus is through this Gopher server. Residents of Greater Columbus can ask for registration forms at their public library. The job listings are in two locations. Choose the "Business Center" for the job listings for Ohio State University. The State of Ohio has its job listings under the "Government Center" menu.

osu.jobs

This newsgroup has jobs at or near Ohio State University.

Oklahoma

The City of Oklahoma City

http://www.ionet.net/~okcpio/index.html

This information server for Oklahoma City includes a list of phone numbers for all departments, including personnel.

Oregon

Oregon Employment Department

http://www.emp.state.or.us/emp1.htm

tn3270://dhrmf.emp.state.or.us

You will need to have your Web browser configured with a TN3270 device (a special kind of Telnet connection) to access these job listings. There is information on obtaining and setting up the TN3270 device, and the service will try to answer questions on this software program as time and staff permit. When you get to the site, type the letter "**G**" and press the **Enter** key at the menu screen (you may have to press Enter to get the menu screen), clear the screen (you should get a message welcoming you to GCICS), and then type "**WORK**" and press the Enter key. Then just follow the instructions. A link to the jobs with the state is available also.

State of Oregon Job Listings

http://www.das.state.or.us/jobs

These extensive state listings are arranged by categories, such as food service and domestic, computing and technology, and education. A search feature is available at the top of the menu, and information on contacting the Employment Department offices is in the file "About the State of Oregon Job Listings." This site can also be reached through the **Oregon Online** Web server at **http://www.state.or.us/** by selecting the link to the Oregon Online Gopher.

All of the following are newsgroups for Portland jobs:

- **pdaxs.jobs.clerical**—clerical positions
- **pdaxs.jobs.computer**—computer sales, support, and programming
- **pdaxs.jobs.construction**—construction
- **pdaxs.jobs.delivery**—delivery jobs
- **pdaxs.jobs.domestic**—help with the home
- **pdaxs.jobs.engineering**—engineering positions
- **pdaxs.jobs.management**—management positions or trainees
- **pdaxs.jobs.misc**—Can you think of something we didn't list?
- **pdaxs.jobs.restaurants**—waitpersons, cooks, bartenders, and so on
- **pdaxs.jobs.resumes**—résumés of persons seeking work

- **pdaxs.jobs.retail**—clothing, hardware, bookstores and so on
- **pdaxs.jobs.sale**—sales positions
- **pdaxs.jobs.secretary**—secretarial positions
- **pdaxs.jobs.temporary**—short-term employment
- **pdaxs.jobs.volunteers**—Help us out!
- **pdaxs.jobs.wanted**—job seekers

Pennsylvania

pgh.jobs.offered

This is a newsgroup for jobs offered in Pittsburgh.

pgh.jobs.wanted

This is a newsgroup for jobs wanted in Pittsburgh.

phl.jobs.offered

This newsgroup covers jobs available in Philadelphia.

phl.jobs.wanted

This newsgroup covers jobs wanted in Philadelphia.

Rhode Island

RIDET—Rhode Island Department of Employment and Training

http://det2.det.state.ri.us/

This service is similar to other state employment offices online, with its easy directions and simple forms. A directory of the employment offices is available online along with links to additional Internet resources. Very well done.

ne.jobs

ne.jobs contract

Both of these newsgroups are for jobs in the New England area.

South Carolina

Job Opportunities in South Carolina

http://www.state.sc.us/jobopps.html

This page includes links to opportunities in the state and federal governments and academe, as well as a link to America's Job Bank. The jobs for South Carolina are divided into major occupational categories, with all job listings displayed under each. These are arranged alphabetically by the city in which they are located, so use the "find" feature in your Web browser to locate keywords. Unfortunately, the list of state employment offices was not online at the time of review. This site can be accessed from the South Carolina State Government page (http://www.state.sc.us/) by scrolling down to "Network and Information Services."

South Dakota

South Dakota's Job Bank-Job Search

http://sd.jobsearch.org/

South Dakota's job bank features simple choices of occupational area, field, and geographic location to get you to the jobs you'd like to see. To apply for a job you see online, fill in the online form, print the screen, and fax or mail it to the office indicated.

Bureau of Personnel, State of South Dakota

http://www.state.sd.us/state/executive/bop/

The Bureau of Personnel handles the hiring for the state along with unemployment and training information. The list of current job openings is updated weekly. State job applications are required to apply for any jobs listed.

Tennessee

memphis.employment

This newsgroup covers jobs in Memphis.

Metropolitan Government of Nashville and Davidson County

http://janis.nashville.org/

Job opportunities with the local government in and around Nashville are listed here.

NBJ's Job Journal, The Nashville Business Journal

http://www.infi.net/nc5/nbj/jj.html

Nashville Business Journal added the job listings from its print journal in response to popular demand. These are classified ads for professional jobs in the Nashville area. If you have any questions or suggestions, e-mail www@infi.net.

Texas

Texas State Government

http://www.texas.gov/

From the very front page, this server links you to numerous job opportunities with many of the state agencies. Among the agencies included are the Texas Employment Commission, the Texas Education Agency, and the Texas State Library.

Texas Employment Commission

http://www.tec.state.tx.us/

telnet://hi-tec.tec.state.tx.us/

The Hi-TEC BBS has a wonderful collection of job listings and other information for job seekers and the unemployed. The Web page still requires you to telnet to the full database. Access to the ALEX database can be found under the job listings. ALEX is not identical to America's Job Bank, so search both databases.

austin.jobs

This is a newsgroup for jobs in Austin.

dfw.jobs

This newsgroup covers jobs in Dallas-Fort Worth.

houston.jobs.offered

This newsgroup is for jobs available in Houston.

houston.jobs.wanted

This newsgroup is for jobs wanted in Houston.

Texas One

http://www.texas-one.org

Although it provides no specific jobs, Texas One does have a search feature that can connect to job-related sites. For example, type the word "employment," and you connect to several sites noted in this book, including E-Span, MedSearch America, Saludos Web Site for Hispanic Employment, Hi-TEC BBS, and the Governor's Job Bank—Texas Employment Commissioner.

tx.jobs

This newsgroup is for jobs in Texas.

ut.jobs

This newsgroup has jobs from the University of Texas, Austin.

utcs.jobs

This newsgroup covers jobs from the University of Texas, Austin, Computer Science Department.

Utah

utah.jobs

This is a newsgroup for jobs in Utah.

Vermont

Department of Employment and Training

http://www.state.vt.us/det/dethp.htm

This link to the Vermont homepage provides job listings, both full and part time, for the entire state. Positions requiring immediate action are posted right on the job page. Listings are divided by the offices servicing them or you can search the entire state. Résumés of Vermont residents searching for work are also listed here for employers to scan.

ne.jobs

ne.jobs.contract

Both of these newsgroups are for jobs in New England.

Virginia

Norfolk Pilot

http://www.infi.net/pilot/classified/

This link for the Norfolk newspaper goes directly to the classified ads. From there you can click on "Help Wanted," business opportunities, "Positions Wanted," advertisements for training and counseling, and other information of interest to job seekers.

Virginian Pilot Online

http://www.infi.net/~pilot/

The Virginian Pilot is based in Hampton Roads and this online version is updated by 8 P.M. the night before each publication is released. The classified ads are sorted by category, and there are additional links to other career services.

Washington

Washington State Information Exchange

http://olympus.dis.wa.gov

gopher://olympus.dis.wa.gov

ftp://olympus.dis.wa.gov

This site for the state of Washington leads you to several different resources. Under the Homepage Washington link there is a subject guide that includes employment information, a link to business resources, and great information on the state government and its departments and agencies.

CareerNet

http://www.careers.org

Career Resources Center, a nonprofit educational organization, announces CareerNet™, the Web's Career Resource Directory. This enormous site includes links to databases of employers, educational opportunities, and self-employment resources, as well as book, periodical, audio and video tape, and computer media bibliographies. CareerNet also includes extensive lists of career counselors, outplacement firms, executive recruiters, temporary and permanent employment agencies, social service agencies, government offices, and even visitor and crisis centers. There's also an up-to-date calender of career-related events. At the time of review, the most developed section of this was the area for Washington.

Job Hotlines for Washington

http://www.gspa.washington.edu/career/Hotlines_welcome.html

These lists of telephone numbers are collected by the Graduate School of Public Affairs at the University of Washington and made available on JILES, the Job/Internship Listing and Employments Service. Use these telephone numbers to get information on available jobs in the Seattle/Kings County area. You will either be connected to a recorded list or to a live person, depending on the hotline.

seattle.jobs.offered

This newsgroup is for jobs available in Seattle.

seattle.jobs.wanted

This newsgroup is for jobs sought in Seattle.

Seattle Online

http://www.pan.ci.seattle.wa.us/

The Public Access Network (PAN) is one of two great public networks for Seattle. Select "Business and Employment" from the front page to access information on local businesses and links to city job openings, regional joblines, and other information with leads to more job listings.

Washington, DC*

West Virginia

City of Morgantown Jobs

http://www.dmssoft.com/city/jobs.htm

Employment opportunities with the city are listed here. For more information, call (304) 284-7405, or access the TDD at (304) 284-7512.

* See *District of Columbia*.

Wisconsin

State of Wisconsin

http://www.state.wi.us/

gopher://badger.state.wi.us/

From the Wisconsin homepage, you can connect to two departments with links to and information on employment opportunities, the Department of Employment Relations, and the Departments of Industry, Labor, and Human Relations.

Department of Employment Relations

http://badger.state.wi.us:70/1/agencies/der/

gopher://badger.state.wi.us:70/11/agencies/der

This department includes a listing of current positions with the state and employment opportunities with local government agencies. Select "Wisconsin Classified Civil Service Employment Opportunities" to access these items. The list is updated weekly.

Wisconsin JobNet, Department of Industry, Labor, and Human Relations

http://danenet.wicip.org/jets/

This database was originally set up by Dane County and includes the listings for the Wisconsin Job Service. The organization is similar to that of the other state job services in that you choose a job category, select a job title, and identify a region of the state. You will be asked to register for this server, but you can arrow past, submit the form, and continue from there. Don't skip over the sample documents, since they are great guides to writing résumés and preparing for an interview, and include a list of 20 basic questions to use in interviewing. Access is also available through the Department of Industry, Labor, and Human Relations (DILHR) under "Related Web Sites."

milw.jobs

This newsgroup covers jobs in Milwaukee.

QTI Professional Staffing's Web

http://www.qstaff.com/qstaff/

QTI Professional Staffing, located in Madison, specializes in placing professional and technical personnel with firms throughout southern Wisconsin. Clients include firms in the computer/MIS and lab areas, as well as other professional fields. Assignments are offered on a long-term, short-term, "contract-to-hire," or direct-placement basis. Although there are no actual listings, QTI describes the types of positions available and requests résumés be e-mailed to QTI. For more information, send regular mail to 5003 University Avenue, Suite 2, Madison, WI 53705; phone: (608) 232-2650; fax: (608) 232-2659; or e-mail: qti@qstaff.com.

West Bend Community Career Network

http://156.46.110.2/

This is a source of great information on choosing and researching a career, on deciding if you need more education, and, finally, for looking at local and state employment opportunities with links to the JobNet and state civil service listings.

Wyoming

Wyoming Employment Resources

http://wyjobs.state.wy.us/

Resources through this service include the state's job bank, the state employment offices, a link to the state's Gopher, and a link to the University of Wyoming's job openings. Job listings are updated daily. Select an area to search or choose the entire state, then select an occupational area to see all jobs listed within it. Use the "find" command in your browser to target keywords on the page.

Personnel Management Division, Dept. of Administration & Information

gopher://ferret.state.wy.us/11/wgov/eb/osd/adm/pmd

Job listings currently available from the state can be accessed through the State of Wyoming Gopher. Listings are arranged in files by major job categories which you will have to page through. To save time, use the "find" button on the Web browser or the "search" command in Gopher to locate keywords in the file.

Resources for More Leads to State and Local Employment Information

Although we have included a great many sites here, we certainly have not listed everything. New services may now be available on state and local servers which were not ready when we were collecting information for this book. If you do not see a resource for the state, region, or city you are interested in, here are some places you can search for links to job listings and leads to related information to assist you. Don't forget about **State and Local Government on the Net** and the **Library of Congress**, which were mentioned at the beginning of this chapter. **HYTELNET** (*Chapter 3*) is also a useful resource to check for freenets and community networks accessible by Telnet.

CityNet

http://www.city.net/

CityNet has listings of information and links to servers in over 113 countries. This is a great way to research locations you are considering moving to or places where you have been offered employment.

CityLink

http://www.neosoft.com:80/citylink/

CityLink specifically lists cities in the United States. You will not find a lot of duplication between this and CityNet, so it is worth examining both lists.

Freenets via the University of Colorado, Boulder

gopher://gopher.Colorado.EDU/
select Other Gophers (*by subject*)
select Free-Nets and Other Community Networks

Freenets and Bulletin Boards via Eastern Kentucky University

gopher://acs.eku.edu:70/
select Explore the Internet
select FreeNets or select Bulletin Boards

Both of these lists provide easy access to a large number of freenets and local community bulletin boards. These are good for finding information about an area and businesses to contact about potential job openings.

CHAPTER 11

Opportunities in Cooperative Education, Internships, and Miscellaneous Work

If you are a college student, your first stop for cooperative and internship information should be your department head or college career center. However, if they don't have anything of interest to you, we have gathered some leads that might help you find a position. In addition to these resources, use the **virtual libraries** to identify other organizations in your major field and contact them about possible work. Use Internet **indexers and search engines** to search the keywords "intern," "internship," "coop," "cooperative education," and "summer" or "temporary" for some other possibilities. Another tip—check college and university Gophers and Web servers in the region where you would like to work to see if they have any possible leads from local organizations. Use The **Mother Gopher** and The **Master List of WWW Servers** to target these sites. Freenets and other resources in **Chapter 10** may also provide some contacts. The major job listing sites included in **Chapter 4** can also be a good source for this type of employment, so search their databases as well.

Job Search Tip: The best way to find work for after college is to begin looking while you are still in college. Look for internships, voluntary work, and opportunities for informational interviews, especially with alumni. Interview for guidance, information, and advice only, but always ask questions like, "If you were starting out today, is there anything you would do differently?" and "How would you advise me to begin my preparations and search?" Internships and volunteer work speak for themselves. You get the inside look at an area of interest, and potential employers get a first-hand, close-up look at you.
Nancy Norton, Career Coordinator, Willamette University, Salem, OR

Internet Sites and Resources for Internships, Coops, and Summer Opportunities

The Entry Level Job Seeker Assistant

http://work1.utsi.edu:8000/~jschmalh/jobhome.html

An excellent source of information on finding an entry-level position through the Internet, this site includes links to companies, online recruiters, and organizations that are willing to hire entry-level employees. There is also a place where your HTML résumé can be linked according to major fields and specialties. Many of the organizations included here will also accept cooperatives and internships. Contact Joseph E. Schmalhofer III at jschmalh@sparc2000.utsi.edu with your questions and comments.

California Polytechnic State University—Summer Jobs

gopher://gopher.calpoly.edu/11/campus_info/campus_serv_and_fac/career_services/jobs/summer

This site has summer employment listings at California Polytechnic State University.

Case Western Reserve University—Part Time/Summer Job List

http://www.cwru.edu/CWRU/Admin/cpp/summer.html

This part-time and summer job listing at Case Western Reserve University is updated regularly.

College of St. Catherine—Internships

gopher://gopher.stkate.edu/11/dept/career/intshp

Internship and job listings arranged in a variety of ways. You can search by department, job title, organization, or full-time versus part-time work.

Cornell University—Internships and Summer Job Services

http://student-jobs.ses.cornell.edu/jobs/

This is a comprehensive, current list of local opportunities and nationwide internships.

Drake University—Summer Jobs

http://www.drake.edu/stulife/carsum.html

Drake University provides this list of summer employment.

Indiana University School of Public and Environmental Affairs—Internships

http://www.indiana.edu/~speacare/intern.html

The Career Center at the Indiana University School of Public and Environmental Affairs provides this site of general information and internship requirements, plus weekly internship listings and program information. For more information, send e-mail to kbazur@indiana.edu.

International Agribusiness Internship Center

gopher://gopher.usu.edu:70/11/USU_Information/cplace/International%20Agribusiness%20Internship%20Center%281IAIC%29

Utah State University lists these internships, which focus on agribusiness. Internship openings are sorted by fields, then position titles. Contact the Center via e-mail at Kirk.Eide@m.cc.utah.edu.

International Internship Directory

gopher://gopher.clemson.edu/11/Academic%20Departments/College%20f%20Liberal%20Arts/International%20Resources/International%20Employment%20Resources%20Gopher/

Clemson University lists its internship programs, including information sources and contact persons.

Job Trak

http://www.jobtrak.com

Your college or university must be a member of Job Trak for you to gain access to the job listings! See if your institution is listed, then call and ask for the password. The site has some tremendous information resources. Those who cannot access the job listings might be able to target the companies listed to ask about opportunities.

Mt. Holyoke College—Internship databases

gopher://gopher.mtholyoke.edu:2772/11/mhc/internship/

Mt. Holyoke College (South Hadley, MA) provides this comprehensive collection of internship listings.

Omaha CareerLink

http://www.omaha.org/careerlink.html

Omaha CareerLink is an information resource maintained by the Applied Information Management (AIM) Institute in cooperation with The Greater Omaha Chamber of Commerce Labor Availability Council's Technical Committee, on behalf of Nebraska's information technology industry. It works to match professionals and college interns with available Nebraska position openings.

Peterson's Guides—Summer Jobs

http://www.petersons.com/career/

Peterson's Guides. Inc., has organized this listing of summer camp opportunities for teenagers.

Russian and Eastern European Internship Opportunities

http://www.indiana.edu/~reeiweb/indemp.html

Internships available in Eastern European countries or in studies of these countries are listed by this Indiana University service.

University of Calilfornia, Berkeley's Work Study Home Page

http://www.uga.berkeley.edu/wsp/

The University of California at Berkeley has divided this site into two areas: "The Work-Study Employer Control Center" for employers only, and "The Work-Study Job Search Facility" for work-study student use. This is a great matching service that enables Berkeley students to locate part-time and summer jobs, internships, and so on in their areas of study. For more information, contact Pandelis Tiritas via e-mail at tiritas@ced.berkeley.edu.

University of Minnesota—Internships

gopher://next1.mrs.umn.edu/11/Student%20Services/Career%20Center/Internships/

Be sure to note the dates in this searchable collection of internships at the University of Minnesota—some 1991 listings are still posted here.

University of Virginia—Internship Services

http://www.virginia.edu/~career/ininfo.html

This is an excellent resource for internship listings for all majors throughout the country (see also EXTERNships at http://www.virginia.edu/~career/exinfo.html). Jim Neumeister was responsible for putting this great resource together for the University of Virginia Office of Career Planning and Placement.

The Whitehouse Fellowships

http://www.whitehouse.gov/WH/WH_Fellows/html/fellows1.html

Information about the White House fellowship program, which spans multiple fields, and the selection process. It includes an application form.

Places to Check for Miscellaneous Opportunities

CollegePro Painters

http://wanda.phl.pond.com/mall/collegepro/

You've seen the signs—these people are painting houses all over the country! Job descriptions, local franchises, and benefits are listed, and they will take your application online. Contact them via e-mail at collegepro@netweb.com.

Peace Corps Home Page

http://www.clark.net/pub/peace/PeaceCorps.html

The Peace Corps has put together this nice home page with information on becoming a volunteer, background on the organization, "Domestic" information, and so on. Need more information? Call Brian P. Lonardo at (202) 606-3912, or send e-mail to blonardo@peacecorps.gov.

Project America Home Page

http://www.mit.edu:8001/activities/project-america/

Project America is a nonprofit organization designed to promote community involvement. For more information, contact the project via e-mail at project-america@4mesa.com, or call (800) 880-3352.

VISTA Web

http://libertynet.org/~zelson/section 1.html

AmeriCorps presents this resource detailing volunteer opportunities in Volunteers in Service to America (VISTA) and related information. It includes information on how to subscribe to the biweekly electronic bulletin *VISTA-L*.

VISTA-L, VISTA On-Line

To subscribe: listserv@american.edu

message: subscribe vista-l yourfirstname yourlastname

Volunteers in Service to America is a national service program aimed at alleviating poverty in America's cities and towns. This biweekly electronic bulletin features immediate openings, program updates, and national service news of interest to career centers, volunteer offices, libraries, professional groups, and potential volunteers. To request an information brochure or application, call (800) 942-2677. The list owners are John Zelson (73302.2504@compuserve.com) and Brian Geoghegan (bgeoghegan@delphi.com).

More Possibilities

The following two sites are unique in their attention to colleges, careers, and the entry-level employment scene. Take a look around or ask your career counselor for help in using the resources they have linked together.

The Catapult, Career Service Professionals Homepage

http://www.jobweb.org/CATAPULT/catapult.htm

JobWeb, The National Association of Colleges and Employers

http://www.jobweb.org

CHAPTER 12

International Opportunities

This chapter features Internet resources for finding employment opportunities in countries other than the United States. Many international recruiters based in one country place employees in several other countries, so you may want to check other countries in a region for references. Many of the larger Internet job sites in **Chapter 4** have some international postings. *Note:* All international sites listing jobs in academe have been placed in **Chapter 7**.

Resources are sorted alphabetically by country or major geographic region. Crossreferences between headings are noted as necessary.

> **Job Search Tip:** Tell stories in your interviews! Be able to briefly and concisely tell the interviewer about your accomplishments by stating the situation, describing the action that was required, detailing the steps you took, and quantifying the results you achieved. For many interviewers, there is no greater indicator of future potential than past success.
> **Judy A. Carbone**, *Career Consultant, Career Development Center, George Mason University, Fairfax, VA*

Services with Listings for Multiple Countries

Careers Online

http://www.ideaf.com/jobs/pps.htm

International employment opportunities are organized by country, many technical jobs are included, but the graphic-intensive list seems to be comprehensive in the variety of fields represented. Contact the Idea Factory, Inc. at (914) 359-7647 or send e-mail to howard@newyork.demon.co.uk.

ICEN-L—International Career and Employment Network

To subscribe: listserv@IUBVM.UCS.INDIANA.EDU

Message: subscribe icen-l yourfirstname yourlastname

This mailing list, maintained at Indiana University, discusses international employment. The archives of the list are not available. For more information, send e-mail to ICENL@ucs.indiana.edu or SMWANG@ucs.indiana.edu.

Postdoc International

Send e-mail to: POST@DOCSERV.SACLAY.CEA.FR

Message: GET INDEX

POSTDOC, based in France, lists academic and research positions of all kinds! Several years ago, some students preparing their Ph.D.s in physics created the organization named "Postdoc

International" that groups together job offerings in laboratory research around the world. These offerings are available to researchers through a computer server. Besides postdoctorates, the server contains offers of permanent positions (senior researcher, laboratory director, and so forth). For more information, send e-mail to one of the following:

Claire Gautherin	GAUTHERI@AMOCO.SACLAY.CEA.FR
Dominique Marchand	MARCHAD@PHNX7.SACLAY.CEA.FR
Etienne Amic	AMIC@AMOCO.SACLAY.CEA.FR
Vincent Vigneron	VVIGNE@SOLEIL.SERMA.CEA.FR

TeleJob

http://ezinfo.ethz.ch/ETH/TELEJOB/tjb_home_e.html

TeleJob is the electronic job exchange board for the Association of Assistants and Doctoral Students of the technological institutes of Zurich (AVETH) and Lausanne (ACIDE). There are plenty of interesting jobs for young academics interested in academe or the business world. The home page is in English with German and French versions available, but many job positions are not listed in English.

Asia/Pacific Rim*

TKO Personnel, Inc

http://www.internet-is.com/tko/

The company recruits for technical positions and companies in Asia, Japan, and the Pacific Rim region. Good information is available for these regions.

Australia**

AK Jobnet, Austin Knight Company

http://www.ak.com.au/akjobnet.html

With an excellent listing of job opportunities in Australia arranged by industry sectors, there is also a section of "blind ads" which protects the identity of both the employer and applicant until such time as they are prepared to meet.

* See also *China*, *Japan*, and *Singapore*.
** See also *United Kingdom*.

aus.jobs

aus.ads.jobs

These newsgroups are for jobs available or wanted in Australia.

Employment Opportunities in Australia

http://employment.com.au/index.html

Jobs available in Australia are arranged by occupation, or you can search by keyword. Listings of companies and consultants included are also searchable. Each listing contains a job description and contact information for applications. Government appointments are also posted here.

Professionals On Line/Employment and Recruitment

http://www.wordsimages.com/emp_rec.htm

Words & Images Printing Ltd. maintains this service, which is based in Australia and provides technical opportunities and a free Web presence for computer consultants. It also links to other Australian and U.K. sites and placement services. Contact the service via e-mail at ian@wordsimages.com.

People Bank

http://www.micromedia.co.uk/ten/

A *free* service for job seekers who can send their information to a database distributed to agencies and employers throughout Australia and the United Kingdom. Agents are used to protect the confidentiality of job seekers registered here. You will need a forms-capable browser to register online.

Austria

at.jobs

This newsgroup covers jobs in Austria.

Canada

These resources have been divided by province and then listed alphabetically by title. Resources with listings for the whole country are at the beginning of the section.

Resources for All of Canada

can.jobs

This is a newsgroup for jobs in Canada.

Career and Placement Services (CaPS)

gopher://chinchaga.ucs.ualberta.ca
/Student Information and Services/Career and Placement Services

The University of Alberta maintains this resource that lists jobs in various fields throughout Canada. It also features career and job search counseling, information on career fairs, and forums.

JobSat

For retrieval instructions: jobsat@hookup.net
Message: help

This Canadian organization's database has thousands of listings from all over North America which can be retrieved by e-mail. Positions range from entry-level to executive. Write for retrieval instructions to jobsatinfo@sx.com.

Jeff Lawrence's Job Page

http://www.qucis.queensu.ca/home/jlaw/job_stuf.html

Jeff was a graduate student in the Imaging Research Labs, Robarts Research Institute, University of Western Ontario. He has put together this list of job sites for himself, and he provides many links to Canadian organizations and recruiters, along with other resources. He is soliciting additions to the list, so any Canadian organization with an Internet site should contact him at jlaw@irus.rri.uwo.ca.

Electronic Job Match International

http://www.tnc.com/ejmi/

This company provides a full spectrum of human resource employment services through all levels of industry and job classifications, with a focus on candidates who are willing to relocate and have transferable skills. Jobs are in all fields, and you can send e-mail to the company to inquire about positions listed. The service will also post summaries of résumés for persons seeking employment, keeping the identity of the job seeker confidential.

Human Resources Development Canada—Metro Toronto

http://www.the-wire.com/hrdc/hrdc.html

This service is sponsored by the St. Thomas Canadian Employment Center (CEC). Job listings are divided by those located in and around St. Thomas and those for the rest of Ontario and Canada. Under each region, the jobs are divided by occupation. Listings are updated daily, but it is suggested you check with your local CEC office for the availability of each position. A list of these offices is available in the "Welcome" area. In addition to the job bank, other information on how to job search, unemployment information, and training programs is included.

ProCom

http://www.flexnet.com/flex/procom/homepg.htm

Professional Computer Consultants Group Ltd. (PROCOM) provides the services of computer personnel on a contract basis. It has been in operation for over 17 years and has offices in both Canada and the United States. Several jobs are listed on its pages, and résumés can be submitted via a form online.

Alberta

ab.jobs

This newsgroup is for jobs in Alberta.

Edmonton FreeNet

telnet freenet.edmonton.ab.ca

login: guest

Job Search Tip: Don't forget the Freenets! Canada has several great freenets that have been established all over the country. Use Peter Scott's **HYTELNET** (another great Canadian product) to find them and put them to good use! I've included some that I have been able to search for job listings, but I know there are more. Look for "Business" or similar headings.

British Columbia

Bridge Information Technology Inc.

http://www.visions.com/netpages/clients/186.html

Located in and serving the Vancouver area, this company has been working since 1991 to assist organizations in finding software engineers, developers, project managers, business analysts, network administrators, and technical writers for contracting/consulting assignments. It also assists organizations in finding permanent staff with those skills. Résumés can be sent by fax, e-mail, or regular mail, and guidelines are on the page. The company also has several positions to be filled listed on its pages.

Prince George Free-Net

telnet freenet.unbc.edu

login: guest

The business and employment section has numerous links to resources for Canadian jobs, and the newsstand includes links to Canadian and world news resources. Guest login is limited to 30 minutes.

Vancouver Regional FreeNet

telnet freenet.vancouver.bc.ca

login: guest

Choose number 4, "Subjects," and then "Employment and Labour" to find good job resources. The news section includes resources for British Columbia. Guest login is limited to 30 minutes.

Victoria Freenet Association (Employment Resources)

gopher://freenet.victoria.bc.ca/11/business

This site links to organizations with job opportunities listed on their Gophers, including some local colleges, companies, and the provincial government. The main menu will lead you to a list of all Gophers in Canada. If you access this from the main menu, select "**Commercial Enterprises**" to view the job listings.

Manitoba

Blue Sky Freenet of Manitoba

telnet winnie.freenet.mb.ca

login: guest, **password:** guest

Set up for the Winnipeg area, this service has some links to job information within the Resource Centre under "Community Support and Development," and more opportunities can be found under "Professional Enterprise and Commerce."

Ontario

Halton Community Network

telnet halinet.shericanc.on.ca

login: guest

Information on the community can be drawn from all over the server, but the government area includes a link into the Human Resources Development Canada and its job listings. Guest login is limited to 60 minutes.

kingston.jobs

This newsgroup covers jobs in Kingston.

kw.jobs

This is a newsgroup for jobs in Kitchener-Waterloo.

Niagara Peninsula Free-Net

telnet freenet.niagara.com

login: guest

This Gopher server has a tremendous amount of business and local information for the Niagara Peninsula area near St. Catherine and Thorold, Ontario, just across the border from Buffalo, New York. Guest login is limited to 30 minutes.

ont.jobs

This newsgroup is for jobs in Ontario.

ott.jobs

This newsgroup has jobs in Ottawa.

Student Employment Services, University of Western Ontario

gopher://gopher.uwo.ca:70/11/.services/ses

Student Employment Services is a division of the University's Student Development Centre. The Job Listing Service is a year-round program that provides hundreds of full-time, part-time, and summer employment listings. The listings highlight positions on campus and in numerous towns and cities across Canada, but the majority of jobs are in the province of Ontario. Most positions require the applicant to contact the employer directly to apply.

tor.jobs

This newsgroup covers jobs in Toronto.

Toronto Free-Net

telnet freenet.toronto.on.ca
login: guest

When you log into this service, you will be asked some questions to determine how your computer is set up. Some sections are not usable by guests, but the business district includes industry profiles from the Canadian government. This is a wonderful resource for career and job exploration information. Guest login is limited to 60 minutes.

Quebec

qc.jobs

This is the newsgroup for jobs in Quebec.

China*

ChinaNet

http://www.asia-net.com
ftp://ftp.asia-net.com
To subscribe: Majordomo@lists.mindspring.com
Message: subscribe china-net

* See also *Asia / Pacific Rim.*

ChinaNet is a clearinghouse for China-related jobs. It publishes job listings via e-mail, FTP, and Web page. All of these services are *free* to individuals looking for China-related jobs. Send questions by fax to (408) 469-0782; e-mail: Jobs@asia-net.com; or letter: ChinaNet, P.O. Box 66855, Scotts Valley, CA 95067.

Denmark

dk.jobs

This newsgroup lists jobs in Denmark.

France

Association Bernard Gregory

gopher://gopher.grenet.fr:700/11/emplois

Job listings are for scientists in France. *All* listings are in French. Archives of the **FROGJOBS** (*see listing in this section*) mailing list are also maintained here.

fr.jobs.offres

This newsgroup covers jobs offered in France.

fr.jobs.demandes

This newsgroup covers jobs wanted in France.

fr.jobs.d

This newsgroup discusses job hunting in France.

Archives of the French Jobs Newsgroups

http://www.loria.fr:80/news/fr.jobs.d.html
http://www.loria.fr:80/news/fr.jobs.demandes.html
http://www.loria.fr:80/news/fr.jobs.offres.html

This site archives the postings of French jobs offered, jobs wanted, and discussion Usenet newsgroups. These are organized by the "Subject" line in the posting, and some postings are quite old. You can search for keywords or even the month of posting using the "find" command in your Web browser.

FROGJOBS—Scientific Jobs in France

To subscribe: Listproc@list.cren.net

Message: subscribe frogjobs yourname

FROGJOBS is sponsored by the French Scientific Mission in Washington. This mailing list is intended to help young French scientists pursuing Ph.D.s or postdoctorates abroad prepare for their professional return to France or Europe by providing complete information on scientific employment, job opportunities, and contacts in public and private research centers. Foreign scientists who plan to work in France will also benefit from FROGJOBS. Archives for this list are kept on the Gopher of The French Association Bernard Gregory, a nonprofit organization founded in 1980 to facilitate young scientists' first employment opportunities. FROGJOBS is moderated. For more information, send e-mail to the list owner, Rene-Luc Benichou at Rene-Luc.Benichou@inria.fr.

Germany

bln.jobs

This newsgroup covers jobs in Berlin and the surrounding area.

de.markt.jobs

This newsgroup is for jobs in Germany.

de.markt.jobs.d

This newsgroup discusses jobs in Germany.

Ireland

ie.jobs

This newsgroup has jobs in Ireland.

The Irish Job Vacancies Page

http://www.internet-eireann.ie/Ireland/irishjobs.html

This service, begun in April 1995, is for individuals looking for work in Ireland. The owners ask that you mention where you found the job listings when you respond. The site links to the Irish Recruitment and Employment Agencies Page, which has additional resources for recruiters in this area. Contact John Feeley at john@exp.ie.

Japan*

iijnet.jobs

This newsgroup posts job openings in Japan.

JapanNet

http://www.asia-net.com

ftp://asia-net.com

To subscribe: Majordomo@lists.mindspring.com

Message: subscribe japan-net

JapanNet is a clearinghouse for Japan-related jobs. It publishes job listings via e-mail, FTP, and Web page. It also maintains and distributes a résumé book of Japanese-speaking professionals. All of these services are *free* to individuals looking for Japan-related jobs. Send questions via e-mail to Jobs@asia-net.com; fax: (408) 469-0782; or mail: JapanNet, P.O. Box 66855, Scotts Valley, CA 95067.

Middle East

Overseas Job Net Info Haus Page

http://www.infohaus.com/access/by-seller/Overseas_Job_Net

Presenting international employment opportunities, particularly in the Middle East, this site includes information on emigration, and living and working in the Middle East, Australia, New Zealand, France, Germany, and the United States.

Netherlands

Avotek Publishing

http://www.universal.nl/jobhunt/

Avotek offers several guides to the European job market, including listings of recruiters in various fields (**Recruiters Network**) and links to international jobs. It also carries some of the better career books published in the United States along with similar guides for Europe. Contact Avotek for more information about anything listed in the site at info@avotek.nl.

* See also *Asia/Pacific Rim*.

Russia

relcom.commerce.jobs

This newsgroup has job postings for Russia and other Eastern European countries.

Russian and East European Institute Employment Opportunities

htttp://www.indiana.edu/~reeiweb/indemp.html

A service of Indiana University, the Institute's listings cover many fields for people who are seeking employment in Russia or Eastern Europe, or for individuals who have expertise in the languages, history, or cultures of these areas.

Singapore*

Career Opportunities in Singapore

http://www-leland.stanford.edu/~chongkee/edb/career.html

This is a service of the International Manpower Programme. All listings are deleted as they are filled. Information on the agency and how to apply for jobs is included as are links to additional job resources and information about Singapore. Very graphic intensive.

South Africa

za.ads.jobs

This newsgroup lists jobs in South Africa.

Sweden

swnet.jobs

This newsgroup covers jobs in Sweden.

* See also *Asia / Pacific Rim*.

Switzerland

United Kingdom

CyberDyne CS Ltd.

http://www.demon.co.uk/cyberdyne/cyber.html

This is a very nice service located in the United Kingdom. In addition to its own services, it includes links to international job listings and some U.S. servers. Many links are arranged geographically by region, including Asia, Australia, and Africa.

Job.net from Computer Contractor

http://www.vnu.co.uk/vnu/cc/

This site is sponsored by a magazine geared to contract opportunities for information technology (IT) professionals. You can search by keywords in the assignment listings or by choosing an agency and looking at its listings. Each assignment has very extensive listings and good information. Additional information on contract work and services is also available.

JobServe

http://www.demon.co.uk/jobserve/

JobServe, a U.K.-based resource, is an e-mail newsletter and Web database of information technology jobs from around the world. Although the majority of listings are in the United Kingdom and related countries, several other international and U.S. opportunities were listed here at the time of review. The database is updated daily, and the e-mail newsletter can be filtered to your specifications. Listings can be viewed by agency, contract versus permanent positions, and what was added on that day. You can subscribe to the e-mail version of the newsletter at subscribe@ jobserve.com., and information on filtering it to just what you want is on the Web site.

Internet Web Recruiting

http://www.internetweb.co.uk/centres/recruitm/recruitm.htm

Have you ever wanted to find a huge list of as many companies and organizations as possible in one place, and then just look for their jobs? In the United Kingdom, this may be that list. Choose your company or organization (the BBC and the British Film Commission are here), check its address, and then click on "Appointments" to see if anything is available.

Price Jamieson

http://www.gold.net/PriceJam/

This U.K. recruiting agency lists jobs in multiple fields. The listings include title, a brief description, and salary, and there are entry-level positions here. Inquiries about jobs can be sent via e-mail once you have viewed the position listings.

The Span Consultancy

http://www.demon.co.uk/cyberdyne/span/span.html

The Span Consultancy, an IT consulting firm in the United Kingdom, maintains this resource. Its major fields are data processing software consulting for AS/400, Oracle, and so on in England. This is a good resource featuring "SpanLink Help" and background material on the Span Consultancy, as well as links to permanent or consulting opportunities. It also offers a good article on what new software consultants should know! For more information, send e-mail to 100441.1607@compuserve.com.

uk.jobs.d

This newsgroup discusses work in the United Kingdom.

uk.jobs.offered

This newsgroup covers jobs offered in the United Kingdom.

uk.jobs.wanted

This newsgroup covers jobs wanted in the United Kingdom.

APPENDIX A

Services for the Experienced Job Seeker

I've come to realize that there are a lot of misunderstandings and misconceptions about some parts of the career service industry, particularly those geared to the more experienced job seeker. We aren't sure what these people do, when we *could* be using them, how we *should* be using them, and for what. I hope this appendix will give you some ideas, improve your understanding of these services, and allow you to make some decisions to help your search for employment.

Executive Search

Most of us are familiar with the slang term *headhunter*, but what do these executive search firms and consultants do, and where do they fit in the job search? We think of recruiters as organizations and people who work to find candidates for jobs, but that is also what an executive search consultant does. What is the difference? They are both recruiters, but it is the *process* of matching employees to employers and the type of contract with the client that differentiates them. Marcia Fawcett, a search consultant, explains: "Some recruiters work on contingency, but I work on retainer. This means I receive payments for professional services rendered. Working on contingency means you are paid for your services only if you fill a position for the employer." Fawcett is principal of The Fawcett Group, consultants in customized executive search and performance management who work with organizations on the "fit-factor" of people within positions and positions within organizations. A piece of her work includes an executive search on behalf of her clients, the goal being to find the ideal employee for the job.

The difference in payment terms that Fawcett noted defines the way in which recruiters search for appropriate candidates. "Contingency recruiters collect large numbers of résumés and hold them in a database so they can identify potential candidates for a client quickly." When a client calls with an opening, the contingency recruiter searches the database, looks over what has been retrieved, checks with the candidates, and refers the best of the résumés to the client in the hope that one will be a good fit with the position the client has in mind. There is little or no consulting with the client, but the search is probably not exclusive to one agency either. Some companies will have several contingency recruiters working to fill the same position.

> Retained search consultants like myself work exclusively with our client to identify the ideal candidate. We research the job field, work with the client to clearly identify the specific skills and features they are looking for in the candidate. We even examine the work environment and culture in the client company. Our goal is to find the best candidate, not just in terms of skills, but also in terms of personality, so the match is successful.

Once the search consultant has the candidate specifications prepared, he or she then creates the search strategy and works to identify where these ideal candidates might be reached. He or she collects résumés of those persons identified as candidates and examines not only the references they provide but tracks down even more references. The search consultant then makes the final decision and forwards the agreed-on number of candidates to the client, generally three or four people, "the real top choices. It takes some time, but the whole idea is the fit of the candidate and the success of the match."

Because of the complexity and cost of the search procedure, this method of recruiting for organizations is usually reserved for the executive employee, hence the term *executive search*. As Marcy notes, "I am primarily looking for candidates with more than ten years experience in the field and who are commanding a salary around $70,000 or higher." Very few people, particularly those who have recently graduated from school, have this kind of experience. They are not among the pool in which the retained executive search consultant is looking. Entry-level job seekers and those with less than ten years experience are more in the realm of the contingency recruiter. It isn't worth forwarding your résumé to these consultants in case something comes up at a later time. Most consultants will glance over it, but if it does not meet any of their current search criteria, it is very unlikely it will be retained.

Perhaps you are someone who meets the broad criteria of the "executive," and you are interested in making a change. How do you get your résumé into this pool where executive search firms will find you? You might consider mailing a cover letter and résumé to some executive search firms to get your name added to their list of potential candidates, but don't expect a lot from this. According to Fawcett, "Most executive search firms will retain résumés of highly qualified candidates. The smaller firms don't have the time and money to maintain these records. I do keep résumés of candidates I have identified in the past who have made a positive impression that I might want to approach again."

So how does someone become a potential candidate? The best way to get your name into the executive search arena is to target search firms who specialize in recruiting for your industry and functional field. You might want to identify a few of the larger firms for contact also. How do you identify the good firms? By recommendation. Ask your friends, colleagues, and former employers about firms with whom they have had contact. Ask them if they have had any experience with a firm and what the quality of service was. If they actually have the name of someone in a firm, contact him or her directly with a cover letter and résumé, and use the name of your mutual contact.

Once you've identified the agencies to whom you want to submit your résumé, prepare your cover letter carefully. Note your interests, geographic preferences, strengths, and pay scale. This letter must summarize you and your employment interests in order to catch the eye of the search consultant. Enclose your résumé, and then go about your usual business. Don't expect a phone call or a face-to-face meeting, and don't call to ask if the letter and résumé were received.

Fawcett says, "If you are someone I want to talk to right now, I will contact you. Otherwise, your letter and résumé will be filed until I have need for them." Don't call and ask for comments on your résumé. That type of request doesn't reflect well on you and it really isn't the role of the search consultant unless he or she is contacting you about a specific search. In that case, you may be given pointers to help tighten up your résumé to match the job specifications.

At all levels, the résumé is a very important tool for your job search. You must have a well-prepared résumé which should be tailored to the job position being applied for. Move away from just listing your job responsibilities and list your accomplishments instead, particularly what problems you've solved. Fawcett's advice: "We refer to it as the **PAR** résumé—what *problem* was addressed, what *action* was taken to resolve it, and what was the *result*. Employers are looking for problem solvers, and this gives them the information they want and lets them see how you will act in their organization."

Two terms keep appearing in this discussion, the *client* and the *candidate*. The definition of these terms may surprise some of you. The client is the organization that contracts the services of the search firm. The client pays all fees associated with the search. You, the job seeker, are the candidate. As the candidate, should you be paying fees to these recruiting firms? *Never*. The days when you would go into an employment agency, pay them a fee, and have them find a job for you are really gone. The employers are the ones paying the fees now for both retained and contingency searches.

Additional reading and research on recruiting can help you decide both how to approach these firms and what to expect in response to your approach. *The Directory of Executive Recruiters* from Kennedy Publications is a great source of information on both retained and contingency recruiting. In addition to the listings of agencies, the directory opens with several good articles about the executive search, what it is, how to use it, and what to look for. Another book for the executive job seeker is *Rites of Passage at $100,000+* by John Lucht. This unique book is geared for the executive job seeker, offering ideas and strategies for approaching the executive job search. Reading Lucht in combination with the articles in the Kennedy directory can give you some good ideas for search strategies. *The National Business Employment Weekly* is also an excellent source of information on all aspects of the job search and should be checked on a regular basis for informative articles and tips to improve your search.

Outplacement

Unless you have been offered outplacement when dismissed from a job, you are probably not familiar with it. In fact, many who have been offered outplacement still have no idea what it is! *Outplacement* is an assistance service for persons leaving employment at an organization to help prepare them for their job search. This idea began in the 1960s as a benefit for senior executives, but it has been gradually spreading through lower-level employees.

Dr. Laurence J. Stybel stresses the true role of the outplacement consultant: "Outplacement consultants do not find you a job. We work with you to prepare you for the job search, helping you to develop the edge which will help you compete effectively for new employment." Stybel is president of Stybel Peabody/Lincolnshire of Boston, an outplacement firm assisting corporate clients with their executive transitions. He also points out that the key word in his statement is *you*. "The outplacement consultants will not write your résumés, set up your appointments, nor establish your networking connections. We work with you to do this for yourself, offering guidance in making decisions and assistance in establishing your search, contact, and interview techniques, but all of the effort is yours and yours alone."

There are three parts to outplacement services:

1. They provide administrative support in the form of office services and work space. You should have a work area and access to a photocopier, a telephone, and possibly a fax machine. A reference library should be available for your use as a part of your job search.
2. They provide psychological support to help you clarify your values, your goals, and even the direction you want to take at this time. As Stybel notes, "Losing your job is a traumatic experience, not just for you but for your family. Your outplacement consultant can help you and your spouse work through this period and begin the adjustment to unemployment and the job search."
3. They provide marketing assistance and guidance, helping you to position yourself in a way that distinguishes you from all other candidates and improves your chances of gaining new employment quickly.

According to Stybel, "Different firms are stronger in some of these areas than in others, so you want to see where a firm stacks up and decide what mix of these three pieces will work best for you."

Outplacement firms identify themselves as either corporate sponsored or retail, meaning they work on contract with an organization or they are available for you to contract their services privately. Is one better than the other? If you are given notice of your dismissal, should you elect to receive outplacement through an agency hired by your company or should you take the money to purchase your own outplacement services? Stybel advises:

> Take the corporate-sponsored outplacement services. This actually saves you money. If you take the payment from the company, you will have to pay taxes on it and then purchase your outplacement support. You will not be able to write off the expenses of your job search on your tax forms until they equal three percent of your gross income. That is a lot of money, and few of us actually meet that requirement. The quality of the outplacement service offered through the company will probably be better than what you can purchase on your own. Human resource professionals talk to each other, and if an outplacement firm is not doing a good job, the word will get around.

You also need to know what level of outplacement is being offered to you, full service or limited.

> Full-service outplacement means the agency and the company are committed to providing support to an outcome, usually meaning new employment. Limited service means they are committed for a specific period of time, anywhere from one month to a year, regardless of the situation.

While the outplacement firms identify themselves as corporate sponsored or retail, you need to be aware that there are also two other classifications for outplacement firms in the market today, those who specialize in consulting and those who specialize in training. "The skills in each firm are different. The training firms will have well-designed programs which are implemented in a consistent manner. The idea can be easily replicated and is useful for large numbers of displaced employees. The consulting firms work to customize the outplacement process to each individual. One approach may work better for you, so you want to be able to choose between them if you can."

What if your organization doesn't offer you outplacement as a part of your severance package? Stybel advises:

> Ask for it. Who should you ask? Human resources would seem to be the most logical choice, but they are not the right people. They are the champions of corporate policy. Any allowance for you may suggest a precedent in policy. The best person to approach to ask for outplacement is the boss who fired you. He or she will be the most receptive to your request although he or she will be the most difficult person to approach. Why will former bosses be so receptive? Guilt has a lot to do with it. They may even arrange to pay for the outplacement from their own budget. This then sets a precedent in the organization and lets them request outplacement if they should be let go. Former bosses actually may not care about you finding new work, but providing support for you will look good to the remaining employees. It's also a recruiting tool, providing assurance to new employees that they will also be supported if they should be let go.

When you discuss outplacement with your employer, there are certain questions you should ask. "Will you receive limited or full-service outplacement? If possible, you want to push for full-service outplacement. Can you meet with the expected counselor? You want to be sure that you can work with this person and that he or she can help you. Ask for a choice of agencies, and then ask your employer or the human resources department to recommend two or three." Finally, if your needs cannot or will not be met by the contracted service, "rattle the cages. Request a new consultant, a new agency, anything you need to assist you at this time." Even if you have received outplacement in the past, request it again. "Don't evaluate an outplacement firm based on your last experience. If last time you worked with a training firm, try for a consulting firm this time." As with any professional service, this is a very personal decision, and only you can say what works and does not work for you.

You have been offered outplacement by your organization, and you are meeting with agencies to select which one you will work with. The place looks good, the administrative services look great, but what else should you be looking for to help you make your final decision?

- If you are meeting with the marketing manager for the agency, all you are probably hearing is how great they are. "Get past this person and request to meet the counselor you will be working with. This is the person you will be relying upon, not the marketing agent."
- You've met with the counselor, and he or she has an obsessive reliance upon networking. "Be on guard. For some people this is the most effective technique to a new job, but it is also the least expensive. If you are shy, it may not work for you at all. It should be only one tool in your job search, not the only tool."
- You're meeting with your counselor, and he or she tells you to sit back, relax, and let him or her search the data-base. He or she has access to the hidden job market. "The job market is not in a database and it is not in their control. It is in your best interest to avoid falling into this trap of complacency and to maintain control of your job search."

Before you make your final choice of outplacement agencies, request the names of other candidates they are currently working with whose cases are similar to yours. Speak with these people and get their impressions of the agency and how it is supporting them.

Stybel suggests asking if the outplacement agency is a member of the Association of Outplacement Consulting Firms International. "This is not an exclusive association, and it is not a guarantee of quality, but the firms who are members have met a certain set of minimum standards which have been established by the association. If a firm is not a member, then what does this say about their commitment to the profession? Anyone can call himself an outplacement consultant or a career counselor, but membership in the association indicates a certain level of dedication to the profession."

More information on outplacement is readily available. *The Directory of Outplacement Firms* from Kennedy Publications is a good resource as a directory of firms and for general information on the industry as well. *The National Business Employment Weekly* frequently carries good articles about outplacement services. Larry and his partner Maryanne Peabody have authored several articles on outplacement services. The few listed here are particularly good and should be available at your local library. If not, ask if they can be obtained by interlibrary loan.

- Stybel, Laurence, and Maryanne Peabody. "Outplacement as Part of Negotiated Settlement." *Massachusetts Lawyers Weekly*, 17 (52): September 18, 1989.
- ———."Advice for the Long Haul: Job Campaigns Helped by Outplacement." *Boston Business Journal*: July 8, 1991.
- ———."Getting Fired and After: As Always, Organization Is the Key." *Boston Business Journal*: June 3, 1991.

In addition to these resources, Outplacement International has published *The High Touch plus High Tech Electronic Job Search Directory*. Edited by Claudia A. Gentner, this book includes many tips, secrets, and anecdotes for job seekers and a wealth of job sources to aid in your search.

Career Counseling after College

You may have been lucky enough to have had the services of career counselors available to you during your college years. You may even have been smart enough to take advantage of these services! Today, most colleges and universities and many high schools have career counseling services for their students. Perhaps you have reached a point in your life where you are thinking about making a change. This might be the time to go back to those career counselors or visit them for the first time. But you are no longer enrolled in school or college. Where do you turn?

While many private counselors are responding to this need for career counseling after college, a number of colleges and universities are also working to meet this demand. Their alumni are returning and asking for assistance, or the communities in which they are located are demanding these services. The School of Continuing Studies at Johns Hopkins University established the Career and Life Planning Center under the direction of Kathleen Bovard to work with adults with job experience who are contemplating making career changes. This office is separate from the career services offered to traditional-age university students and serves three distinct populations: the continuing education students and alumni of the university, faculty and staff of the university, and professionals in the community who either desire a change or have been forced into a change by circumstances.

> What might you expect from a career counselor, especially as an older job seeker? According to Bovard, counseling begins with an initial information-gathering meeting between the client and the counselor. We discuss the client's background, establish a plan of action, and set some goals for each session. Career counseling is a very dynamic process. We want to know where clients, job seekers, have been, find out some ideas as to where they might like to move, and set up a plan of action to keep them moving forward with their career planning. Self-assessment is often the first step in the process. Clients may benefit from taking one or more standardized vocational assessment tools such as the Strong Interest Inventory or the Campbell Interest and Skill Survey to help them identify different career options based on their skills and interest. Eventually we lead clients to a point where they can make the decisions necessary to move on with their careers or even to change them.

When Johns Hopkins established this separate career center, it acknowledged the fact that the older person entering career counseling has different needs than the traditional-age college student. "Working with an experienced adult client can be much more complex than advising the typical college student. There are often personal and family factors, as well as financial demands, which have to be considered now. They have a job history and a career, and if they have recently lost their job, their self-esteem may be low and their anxiety high." Many of the clients working with this office are not in search of résumé-preparation assistance. "While we help clients write résumés and prepare for job interviews, our primary services are the self-assessment and decision-making processes. We help our clients work through these important steps so they can take the next step in their job search, whether it is to continue searching in their chosen field or to make a change and try something new."

In all of this, Bovard is referring to the client as the person she is working with: "The client is the person who has been laid off or is seeking career guidance. Many companies do not provide career counseling for their displaced employees." If you feel you might need the services of a career counselor, where can you begin looking for help? "If you are a college graduate, call the career center at your college and see if they might be able to help you find reciprocal services at another college or university close to you. Many colleges and universities may be willing to provide assistance at no cost if they have established a reciprocal relationship with your alma mater. Otherwise, call your local colleges, community colleges, and universities. Check with their career centers about providing these services. If they don't, ask if they could recommend someone in the area. You might also contact university continuing education offices with similar questions. Some community organizations may have career counseling services available too. Check your local phone book for more information about these types of services."

If you decide to work with a private career counselor, you can pick up the local phone book and find any number of people calling themselves career counselors in the Yellow Pages. Bovard suggests using the following checkpoints as one way to help evaluate their services:

Ask if they have been certified by the National Board for Certified Counselors. This organization has a specific certification program for career counselors, and if you call the national office, they will give you the names of certified counselors in your area. Many states license counselors, and, if your state is one of these, find out if the person you are talking with has been licensed. The counselor may be licensed by the state but not certified by the National Board or vice versa. Either credential assures that your counselor has had a minumum number of years of supervised counseling experience, is at the master's degree level, and has successfully passed a comprehensive written examination. You will also want to ask if they are members of the National Career Development Association. While it's not a guarantee of quality, membership does show a commitment to the profession. Finally, realize that the relationship between you and your career counselor is a personal one. If you are not happy with your counselor, find another one. It may be something simple like you don't like his or her style, but that can be a very big deal."

If you are considering making a career change, the self-assessment and decision-making process can be the most difficult part. To get an idea of the process, read some of the great books on the subject that are available at your local public library. Richard Bolles' book *What Color Is Your Parachute?* is probably the most highly recommended and can help you begin thinking about the next step in your job search or in your career. Tom Jackson's book *Not Just Another Job* will introduce you to new ideas for mapping your career path and applying your skills to new or alternate employment areas. *The National Business Employment Weekly* regularly carries articles about changing careers. Your local public library or college career center may have copies you can read.

APPENDIX B

Using Dial-Up Bulletin Boards

Beyond the Internet are several other networks and resources you can access that have information useful to your job search. America Online, CompuServe, and the other commercial service providers all offer their users special areas dedicated to job listings and career information. Other electronic networks also have areas for job postings.

This list is dedicated to employment resources on dial-up bulletin boards (BBS) maintained by different organizations all over the United States. Many of these are free, and many offer you more than just a place to look for a job. Some of them even have Internet access, and we've tried to note them here.

Harold Lemon is one of the evaluators for resources included in this book. He works as a computer systems analyst in the San Francisco Bay Area, usually on short-term contracts, and has become an expert at finding work and dealing with contract employment. Like so many others on the Internet, he has taken the list of good resources he has found and put it up for the rest of us to try. That is really what drives the Internet—the sharing of information and the cooperation between the users. As many others have said to him in the past: *Thanks, Harold!*

Harry's Job Search BBS & Internet Hot List

Introduction to the List

During my job search, I ran across several BBS and Internet sources that contained job listings from all over the country. I finally decided to put together the following list of the ones I felt would be the most helpful to those people who are still looking or have just started looking for a job. I know that it would have made my job search a lot easier if I had had all this information in the beginning. I will try to keep it updated as much as possible. The list is now sorted by state, where possible, to make it easier to find a BBS near you.

Should you come across a job-related BBS that you feel would be beneficial to other job seekers, let me know what and where it is and I will add it to the list. You can leave e-mail for me on **D.I.C.E. National Network**, send e-mail to my Internet address **(hlemon@netcom.com)**, or send regular mail to:

Harold Lemon
3241 San Carlos Way
Union City, CA 94587 USA

This release and future updates to this list may also be obtained by

1. Calling **Online Opportunities BBS** at (610) 873-7170
2. Sending Internet e-mail to **hotlist@jobnet.com**

* Copyright © 1995 by Harold Lemon

3. Reading it on the World Wide Web at **http://www.wpi.edu/~mfriley/jobguide.html** or **http://rescomp.stanford.edu/jobs.html**
4. Watching for it on the **misc.jobs.misc** Usenet newsgroup

If you can't retrieve it from any of these services, I can send you a print copy. Send me a check or money order for $5.00 to the above address. That fee covers my expenses for making a photocopy and sending it to you.

My very sincere thanks go out to all those wonderful people who contributed sources that were added to the list.

Good luck in your job search!

Format of the Listings

BBS Name **Telephone Number** **Max Baud**
Location
Comments

Listings

SBA-Online (800) 697-4636 9600
Internet: telnet sbaonline.sba.gov
gopher://www.sbaonline.sba.gov

Small Business Administration BBS. Loaded with information. No fee required. Internet e-mail.

Walt Disney Productions

The Disney Applicant Information System (DAISY) has been discontinued; however, ***you can still send your résumé to their Internet e-mail address (resumes@disney.com.)***. They are currently accepting résumés for technical, computer science, and software positions.

AVADS-BBS (DoI) (800) 368-3321 9600

U.S. Department of the Interior Job Announcements. The Automated Vacancy Announcement Information Center provides information on job vacancies from ten bureaus at the Department of the Interior. No fee required. Also accessible via FedWorld BBS Gateway (DD132).

Career Link, Inc. voice (800) 453-3350 2400
Phoenix, AZ

Job bank of U.S. and overseas jobs. Fee required. Updated weekly. Must call for user i.d., password, and 800 number for accessing BBS.

The Bizopps Connection (310) 677-7034 9600
California

An information service with searchable database with listings of business and franchise opportunities, venture capital sources, and money-making opportunities. Fee required.

Computer Department EIC (310) 421-6089 9600
California

Computer consulting/secretarial service. No fee required.

D.I.C.E. National Network

Sunnyvale, CA	(408) 737-9339	9600
Newark, NJ	(201) 242-4166	9600
Des Moines, IA	(515) 280-3423	14400
Chicago, IL	(708) 782-0960	9600
Dallas, TX	(214) 782-0960	9600
Boston, MA	(617) 266-1080	9600

Internet: Telnet dice.com
ftp://dice.com
http://www.dice.com

Excellent for nationwide contract and permanent data processing jobs. Job postings from 200+ agencies. Updated several times daily. No fee required.

ouT therE BBS (408) 263-2248 9600
San Jose, CA

Contract and permanent job listings for San Francisco Bay Area. No fee required. Updated every two days.

Contractors Exchange (415) 334-7393 14400
San Francisco, CA

BBS for construction-type contractor jobs. Few data processing jobs. Updated daily. No fee required.

Environet (415) 512-9108 2400
California (415) 512-9120 28800

Job openings with Greenpeace. Updated daily. Most jobs are in U.S. with a few in other countries. No fee required.

Global Trade Net (415) 668-0422 9600
California

International trade forum. Help for starting a new business. Bid and selling areas. No fee required.

Career Connections (415) 903-5815 14400
Los Altos, CA (415) 903-5840 2400
Internet: Telnet to career.com
New grads: Telnet to college.career.com

Worldwide computer and noncomputer job listings by the hiring companies. No fee required.

DP NETwork (Toner Corp.) (415) 788-7101 9600
San Francisco, CA (415) 788-8663 2400

Good source of data processing jobs for the San Francisco/Sacramento area. Also, the JOBS-NOW echo in the Information Services section has listings of data processing jobs nationwide. Updated daily. No fee required.

Look Smart (510) 794-7381 9600
Fremont, CA

A service of the Alameda County Library to help San Francisco Bay area jobseekers. This BBS contains indexes of business directories, reports, and salary surveys with many more new features to come. No fee required.

HRCOMM (510) 944-5011 14400
Pleasant Hill, CA

HRCOMM is an exclusive online network for human resource professionals. It has products and services, skills/registry, résumé uploads, job postings, and much more. No fee required.

Bust Out BBS (510) 888-1443 9600
Hayward, CA

JobNet echo carrying job listings and information nationwide. Fee required.

Lee Johnson International (510) 787-3191 9600
Crockett, CA

A search firm specializing in employer-paid recruiting and placement. No fee required.

Employment Board (619) 689-1348 9600
San Diego, CA

JOBS-NOW echo and employment information for the San Diego area. No fee required.

Mushin BBS (619) 452-8137 14400
San Diego, CA

Contains various job listings for the San Diego area. No fee required to browse job listings.

Pacific Rim (619) 278-7361 19200
San Diego, CA

Contains job listings from Usenet newsgroups and Fidonet. Internet e-mail access. Fee required.

InfoMat BBS (714) 492-8727 9600
San Clemente, CA

Job opportunity and franchise information. Carries several echoes, such as JobNet, Laran Communications, and Rime and Intelec job forums. No fee required.

The Resume File (805) 581-6210 2400
Simi Valley, CA

A very comprehensive collection of nationwide job listings. No fee required. Also has job-related areas with job-hunting info and tips. Small Business Administration and federal government job information.

Federal Jobline (818) 575-6521 2400
Los Angeles, CA

Federal Job Information Center operated by the Office of Personnel Management (OPM) contains federal job listings and information for the Western region. No fee required.

OPM Mainstreet (202) 606-4800 9600
Washington, DC

Operated by the Office of Personnel Management, contains a variety of information for government employees but is available to anyone. It also has a gateway to the other Federal Job Information Centers. No fee required.

CAPACCESS Career Center (202) 785-1523 14400
Washington, DC
Internet: *Telnet to* cap.gwu.edu, *login as* guest *with password of* visitor.
at prompt, type go careers *or* go jobs
http://www.capaccess.org

The National Capital Area Public Access Network, Inc. contains computer and noncomputer job information from the National Science Foundation, National Institute of Health, Public Health Service, Department of the Interior, Department of Defense, and U.S. Department of Agriculture. No fee is required.

ALIX (202) 707-4885 14400
Washington, DC
Internet: *Telnet to* alix.loc.gov 3001

The Automated Library Information eXchange (ALIX) is run by the Federal Library and Information Center Committee as a service to the federal library community. Contains current federal library job openings, federal library job hotlines, and federal government job hotlines and BBS. No fee required.

U.S. Department of Labor (212) 219-4784 9600
Washington, DC

Downloadable files of federal job opportunities nationwide. No fee required.

Society for Tech. Comm. (703) 522-3299 9600
Washington, DC

Society for Technical Communications operates this BBS. *For technical writers only*. Job service and freelance registry. Job listings available only to verified STC members. No fee required.

Census Personnel Board (800) 451-6128 2400
Washington, DC

Operated by the U.S. Department of Commerce, Bureau of the Census. Job listings for Suitland, MD only. No fee required.

Careers BBS (305) 828-5697 9600
Florida
Fidonet: 100:1260/100

National echo conferences, online forums, Netmail access. Local and national areas for reading and posting employment classifieds. No fee required.

Vanguard Chronicle Network (305) 524-4411 14400
Florida

Carries job listings for hospital positions in nursing, administration, and so on. Résumé uploads. Business employment, community, and health information. Requires special software which can be downloaded on first call. No fee required.

Advanced R&D's Pipeline (407) 894-0580 9600
Orlando, FL

Contains job listings in various job types for the Midwest and Southeast. No fee required. Résumé upload available.

FORTUNE Consultants of Or (407) 875-1028 9600
Maitland, FL

Contains job listings in various occupations. No fee required. Résumé upload available.

J-Connection

Clearwater, FL	(813) 791-0101	9600
Washington, DC Metro	(703) 379-0553	9600
Atlanta, GA	(404) 662-5500	9600

Contains national job listings in data processing. Skill registration. No fee required. Downloadable job files.

OPM Atlanta (404) 730-2370 2400
Atlanta, GA

Federal Job Information Center Atlanta operated by OPM has online job search facility and downloadable files for all regions. Very nice! No fee required.

FirstStep (404) 642-0665 14400
Atlanta, GA

Contains job listings in approximately 100 occupations nationwide. Fee required. Internet e-mail and Usenet newsgroups. Résumé upload is also available.

JOBBS (404) 992-8937 2400
Roswell, GA

Operated by Alpha Systems, Inc., contains job listings in all areas and all positions. Also has listings of recruiting firms and companies. No fee required.

Georgia Online (404) 591-0777 9600
Atlanta, GA

Operated by Foster Employment Services. Has job listings, résumé database, Help Wanted USA services. Also has Internet e-mail and Usenet newsgroups. Fee required.

Index Systems TBBS	(404) 924-8414	28800
Atlanta, GA	(404) 924-8472	28800
	(706) 613-0566	28000

Internet: *Telnet to* indexBBS.is.net *or* indexBBS.com

Job networking. Job listings of high-tech jobs, job hotlines, and software for job seekers. Fee required for expanded access.

RHost (404) 392-9164 2400
Atlanta, GA

Operated by Robert Half of Atlanta. Contains job listings in all areas. Updated daily. No fee required.

FJOB BBS (912) 757-3100 9600
Macon, GA
Internet: *Telnet to* fjob.mail.opm.gov

Federal Job Information Center operated by OPM. Contains federal job listings and information for all of the United States. No fee required.

Doc's Place BBS (309) 682-6560 28800
Illinois

Lists employment opportunities in various fields in the medical technical area. No fee required.

ECCO*BBS

Chicago, IL	(312)-404-8685	14400
New York (metro), NY	(212) 580-4510	14400

The Chicago system lists computer contract and permanent jobs for Chicago and Illinois areas only and has free Internet e-mail. The New York system lists computer and related contract and permanent jobs for most of the East Coast. No fee is required for either system.

Chicago Syslink	(708) 795-4442	28800
Berwyn, IL	(708) 795-4485	28800
	(708) 795-4456	14400

Fidonet:1:115/622

Lists Help Wanted USA job listings nationwide, all positions. Fee required. Internet e-mail.

Job & Opportunity Link (708) 690-9860 9600
Winfield, IL

Home of JOB-LINK and RESUME-LINK. Jobs in all areas are downloadable. Also carries information from FRANCHISE-LINK, OPP-LINK, and MERCH/SERVICE-LINK. No fee required.

Logikal Career Connection (708) 420-0424 9600
Illinois

Data processing professionals on W2 or 1099 status. Special software required to communicate which can be downloaded on first call.

Radiocomm (708) 518-8336 14400
Park Ridge, IL

An online network for people in the radio broadcasting field. Job information and industry news. Fee required.

DP JOB WORKS (219) 436-9702 14400
Fort Wayne, IN

Contains data processing/management information system/information system (DP/MIS/IS) national job listings in downloadable files. Updated weekly. Résumé upload available. No fee required.

Career Systems Online (413) 592-9208 2400
Chicopee, MA

Variety of jobs, including data processing nationwide. Résumé uploads available. No fee required.

National Technical Search (413) 549-8136 14400
Amherst, MA

Operated by Allen Davis & Associates. Has national job listings plus forums and career guides. No fee required. Updated every Monday.

Employment Connection (508) 537-1862 28800
Leominster, MA

Lists various job positions in all areas, mainly on the East Coast. No fee required.

The Employment Line BBS (508) 865-7928 14400
Sutton, MA
Compuserve: 71756. 3471

Various job opportunities in all areas. Mostly on the East Coast. Must submit résumé and $25.00 fee for full registration.

Careers On-Line (508) 879-4700 9600
Framingham, MA

Computer World newspaper's BBS with listings of data processing jobs nationwide. No fee required. Online résumé board.

Network World Online (508) 620-1178 9600
Framingham, MA
Internet: network@world.std.com

Operated by *Network World* magazine. Contains job listings and information and advice on career-and job-related issues. No fee required.

VIEWlogic Personnel Dept. (508) 480-8769 9600
Marlboro, MA

VIEWlogic Systems, Inc. human resource and employment opportunities BBS contains career openings for California and Massachusetts, résumé uploads, benefits information, and human resource department contact information. No fee required.

NFB Net (410)-752-5011 9600
Baltimore, MD

Sponsored by the National Federation for the Blind. Provides information and training materials to assist the blind. The services that are offered are designed to help both the job seeker and employer. No fee required.

Detroit Service Center (313) 226-4423 9600
Detroit, MI

U.S. Office of Personnel Management operates this BBS. Contains federal job opportunity lists and information for the Detroit region. No fee required.

Delight The Customer (517) 797-3740 9600
Hudsonville, MI (616) 662-0393 9600

Focused on customer service, training, and help desk professionals. Job information for manager level and above. Fee required.

Kasta, James and Assoc. (612) 536-0533 14400
Edina, MN

Operated by Kasta, James and Associates, contains job listings for management information system and engineering in the Twin Cities metro area. No fee required.

Computer Career (704) 554-1102 14400
Charlotte, NC

Operated by EDP Professionals, Inc.. Specializes in DP [data processing] jobs nationwide. No fee required.

Nebraska Online (800) 392-7932 9600
Omaha, NE

State of Nebraska state job listings and other state related info. No fee required.

Careers First, Inc. of NJ (609) 786-2666 2400
Cinnaminson, NJ (609) 786-2667
(215) 676-5528

Employment opportunities of computer and miscellaneous positions. Updated weekly. Résumé upload and job-hunting tips available. No fee required.

Praedo BBS (609) 953-0769 9600
New Jersey

Federal job listings and job listings for senior executives and CEOs. Also features tips on résumé writing. No fee required.

INFO-Line (908) 922-4742 14000
Oakhurst, NJ

Contains job information mainly from pharmaceutical companies. Résumé upload available. No fee required.

The Job Bank (315) 449-1838 19200
Jamesville, NY

Operated by Information Systems Staffing, Inc. (ISSI). Contains DP/MIS/IS contract and permanent job listings nationwide. Résumé upload and QWK Mail offline read job listing files is available. No fee required.

Enginet (513) 858-2688 9600
Fairfield, OH

Referral service for engineers. Job bank is an online job placement system that aids engineers and employers in meeting job needs. Also has Internet e-mail and Usenet job newsgroups.

Unicom Info Service (614) 538-9250 14400
Columbus, OH (614) 538-0548 28800
(614)-538-0549 19200

Information exchange for entrepreneurs, managers, and business professionals. Trade leads and other business information. Usenet newsgroups and Internet e-mail. Fee required for expanded access.

Access America (918) 747-2542 14400
Tulsa, OK

Carries job-related Usenet newsgroups and Fidonet echoes of jobs in different areas. Also has Internet e-mail and résumé uploads. No fee required.

JOBS-BBS (503) 281-6808 9600
Portland, OR

The ultimate source for all jobs nationwide. Home of the moderator of the JOBS-NOW echo. No fee required. Updated three to four times daily, Monday through Friday, and five to six times daily, Saturday and Sunday.

Online Opportunities (610) 873-7170 14400
Philadelphia, PA
Internet: *Telnet to* jobnet.com

Excellent source of all jobs nationwide. Some fees required. Updated weekly. This is a Help Wanted USA echo and carries career information, programs, voice job hotlines, and so on. "Phila." résumé database is *free* and marketed in the Philadelphia Tri-State area (eastern Philadelphia, southern New Jersey, and northern Delaware) only.

OPM FEDJOBS—Philly (610) 580-2216 14400
Philadelphia, PA

Operated by the U.S. Office of Personnel Management, this BBS is the source for open federal government jobs and training schedules for all of the United States. No fee required. Updated daily. PC PURSUITable.

Legal Genius (610) 695-9689 9600
Philadelphia, PA
Internet e-mail: justice@locke.ccil.org

Legal files, law school outlines, message areas, and résumé bank. No fee required.

Condell Online (803) 686-3465 2400
Hilton Head, SC

Condell Online contains job listings for people in the title insurance industry. Free access to the "Employment Exchange"scction is available for nonmembers. Résumé upload is available.

Techtips BBS (615) 662-5712 14400
Nashville, TN

Contains biomedical/imaging service forum with job-related files. Also has national job-related echos, Internet e-mail, and newsgroups. Fee required.

Job Trac BBS (214) 349-0527 2400
Dallas, TX

Job listings, résumé uploads, and job forums in all areas for the Dallas-Fort Worth area. No fee required.

Matrix Resources (214) 239-5627 9600
Dallas, TX

Contains various computer job listings for permanent and contract positions. No fee required. Résumé upload available.

Analysts Int'l Corp. (214) 263-9161 9600
Dallas, TX

Operated by AIC. Contains computer job listings for contract positions in the Dallas-Fort Worth area. No fee required.

Digital X-Connect BBS (214) 517-8443 14400
Plano, TX (214) 517-8315 14400

Home of the JobNet echo. Contains job opportunity lists nationwide and job-related information. Also, has BBS listing of all BBS that carry the JobNet echo nationwide. No fee required.

Executive Connection (214) 306-3393 9600
Dallas, TX

Career, employment, and business management. Local and national job openings in all occupations.

Job Bulletin Board (214) 612-9925 9600
Plano, TX

Contains job listings in data processing. No fee required. Résumé upload available.

Window on State Gov't BBS (800) 227-8392 9600
Austin, TX (for TX only)
Internet: *Telnet to* window.texas.gov

This BBS, operated by the Texas State Comptroller's office, contains a variety of information and also provides a gateway to other state BBS (from Main Menu, select option 6, then option 3) such as, Hi-TEC BBS (Texas Employment Commission) and TEC-HR BBS (Texas Education Agency). No fee required.

Texas Education Agency (512) 475-3689 9600
Austin, TX

Operated by the Texas Education Agency Human Resources Division. Contains Texas state government job listings in Austin. No fee required.

hi-TEC BBS (512) 475-4893 14400
Austin, TX

The Governor's Job Bank contains information on job-placement services, unemployment compensation, and employment law. It also has job listings from various Texas state agencies. No fee required. Also accessible via Window on State Government BBS.

Corpus Christi On-Line (512) 850-8255 14400
Corpus Christi, TX

Contains computer and noncomputer job listings for Corpus Christi, San Antonio, and national and international job markets. Also, job lists from Internet newsgroups. Fee required.

San Antonio On-Line (210) 520-8015 14400
San Antonio, TX

Contains computer and noncomputer job listings for Corpus Christi, San Antonio, and national and international job markets. Also, job lists from Internet newsgroups. Fee required.

Turning Point (512) 219-7848 14400
Austin, TX (512) 703-4400 16800
Fidonet: 1:382/106
Internet: info@point.com

Carries job listings from Usenet newsgroups. Internet e-mail. Fee required.

Computer Job BBS (817) 268-2193 2400
Bedford, TX

Operated by Data Processing Careers, Inc. Job listings for Texas only. No fee required.

City of Ft Worth Info Ctr (817) 871-8612 2400
Fort Worth, TX

The City of Fort Worth Public Information Center contains job listings in various areas and miscellaneous information for the Fort Worth arca. No fee required.

FedWorld (703) 321-8020 9600
Springfield, VA
Internet: *Telnet to* fedworld.gov (192.239.93.3)
ftp://ftp.fedworld.gov (192.239.92.205)
http://www.fedworld.gov

FedWorld: National Technical Information Service has federal government job listings worldwide. Also has gateway to 100+ other government BBS. No fee required.

SAK Consulting BBS (703) 715-1016 28800
Reston, VA

Lists federal job openings, specialized search program, and national and overseas listings. Fee required.

The AD Connection (804) 978-3927 2400
Charlottesville, VA

Contains classified ads and federal government job listings. No fee required.

Virginia Employment Comm. (804) 371-6521 9600
Charlottesville, VA

The Virginia Employment Commission is an ALEX system that contains military, federal, state, international, and regional job openings in all areas. Auxillary aids and services are available to individuals with disabilities. No fee required.

Nat'l Software Employment (800) 860-7860 14400
Burlington, VT

Contains a job database of over 15,000 listings from over 17 U.S. cities. Fee required.

WASNET (202) 606-1113 9600
Washington (voice) (202) 606-1848

Contains federal job information and recruitment-related matters. Must call voice number first and leave first and last name plus a password of up to eight characters. No fee required.

Online Info Services (206) 253-5213 28800
Vancouver, WA

Contains job listings from Fidonet, ESN (Enterprise System Network), and Usenet. Also has job broker profile database. No fee required.

Employer's Network (206) 475-0665 19200
Tacoma, WA (206) 471-7575 14400

Contains Internet job listings, federal job listings, local job listings (Pierce County), résumé programs, and résumé database. No fee required.

Exec-PC BBS (414) 789-4210 9600
Wisconsin

E-Span Job Search access. No fee required to access Job Search door. Large variety of job listings in all areas.

Career Connections (414) 258-0164 2400
Wauwatosa, WI

Employment opportunities for job seekers and employers. No fee required.

Project Enable (304) 759-0727 28800
Cross Lanes, WV
E-mail address: enable@rtc.2.icdi.wvu.edu

Sponsored by The President's Committee on Employment of People with Disabilities. Contains job information and help-guides for people with disabilities. No fee required.

APPENDIX C

Online Career Development Resources

One of the truly great features of the Internet is the sharing of information and resources between organizations and the ability for anyone with Internet connectivity to access all of this. This appendix provides a list of sites and resources to assist you with preparing for your job search and for conducting research on an organization before you go in for your interview. Many college and university career centers are making their guides and basic information available on the Internet, and you can benefit from this. There is also a number of great sites with information to help you find out more about the places you are about to apply to or to interview with, and the better prepared you are the better you will appear.

Career Counseling and Placement Services

Most of these are links to career resource and counseling centers at colleges and universities, but some other organizations are also available.

The Catapult, Career Service Professionals Homepage

http://www.jobweb.org/CATAPULT/catapult.html

The Catapult is the springboard to the frequently visited places of Career Service Professionals and other great souls. The Catapult is maintained by the National Association of Colleges and Employers, and it contains more than 200 links to career and employment resources. There is great information to begin researching companies and organizations you might want to check for employment opportunities. If you have questions, you can contact Charette at LJChar@mail.wm.edu.

JobWeb, The National Association of Colleges and Employers

http://www.jobweb.org

JobWeb is intended to be "the electronic gateway to career planning and employment information, job-search articles and tips, job listings, and company information for college students, recent graduates, and alumni." There are significant resources for college career services and employment professionals, including career and employment information, training, and services sponsored by the National Association of Colleges and Employers, formerly the College Placement Council. A great resource for researching potential employers.

Hiatt Career Center, Brandeis University

http://www.brandeis.edu/hiatt/hiatt_home.html

Frank Fessenden, one of the resource evaluators for this book, put together this site for his career center at Brandeis University in Waltham, MA. His site includes links to unique Internet resources to aid in your job search, as well as materials he has developed to assist the students at Brandeis.

Getting Past Go: A Survival Guide for College Graduates

http://lattanze.loyola.edu/MonGen/

This colorful site is an easy guide to life after college, including such mundane information as insurance, figuring out where the best jobs are, staying connected after college, and job hunting. Very easy to follow and read, it is sponsored by Monumental General Insurance Group. Chris Webb is the maintainer (cwebb@lattanze.loyola.edu).

Graduate Horizons, Career Information

http://www.gold.net/arcadia/horizons/

This site is an excellent resource for the new graduate seeking work in the United Kingdom and for other information on choosing a career. It can be slow at times, but the information is worth the wait.

Discovery Home Page

http://w3.ag.uiuc.edu/AIM/Discovery/home.html

The AIM Lab at the University of Illinois, Urbana-Champaign maintains this unique site where colorful graphics provide information, ideas, and exercises to highlight important career exploration concepts. Take a tour of several "asynchronous" learning modules, including "Networking," "Career," and Discovery's "Virtual City." Learn more about basic career concepts, and perhaps learn a bit more about yourself in the process. Highly recommended! If awards were given, Discovery would win a few. Send questions or suggestions to aimlab@uiuc.edu.

Career Information for Various Disciplines

Are you unsure of what might be possible with your degree? Do you feel your career has come to a standstill? These various links might help you find new ideas on how to proceed or progress further.

Career Services Major Resource Kit

gopher://gopher.udel.edu/11/.dept/carserv/MRkit

The University of Delaware has a great service which includes information on careers for several majors. The question "What can I do with a major in..." is answered with examples of job titles, job descriptions, major employers, and citations for more information.

Career Development Resources, American Mathematical Society

http://www.ams.org/committee/profession

This service is only one of many offerings from The American Mathematical Society's E-Math Information Service. It has several articles on career choices for mathematicians, particularly in nonacademic fields.

Physics Careers Bulletin Board

http://aip.org/aip/careers/careers.html

Sponsored by the American Institute for Physics (AIP), six physicists are featured each month. Each is from a different job sector, and they can answer your questions about how they got where they are, what courses and degrees you need, and how to combine physics with your other career interests. You can access the conference forum, read a short biography, and post questions to the physicist(s). The AIP is a good site for learning about careers related to physics, but does *not* include job listings. For more information, send e-mail to Kelli Miller: kmiller@aip.acp.org.

The Scholarly Societies Project

http://www.lib.uwaterloo.ca/society/overview.html

This site contains links to all of the scholarly and professional academic societies with servers on the Internet. Many organizations include job listings for their members, and these might be useful to scan for ideas of careers and/or professions to pursue. Check for listings of "professional development," "career resources," or "member services." A service of the Library at the University of Waterloo (Canada). This server can be very busy, so off-hours use is recommended.

Assistance for Writing Résumés, Interviewing, and Other Tasks

More resources are available from the various career counseling and placement services at the Catapult and from JobWeb.

AAA Resume Service

http://www.infi.net/~resume/

This site is provided by a Greensboro, NC, résumé-writing firm. In addition to information about its own services, the site provides great information on interviewing and choosing a résumé service, and a weekly "hints and tips" page. Substantial links to additional career services and job sites on the Internet are included. For a fee the service will write your résumé for you.

OWL—Online Writing Lab, Purdue University

http://owl.trc.purdue.edu/

This online information resource was set up to help with writing all types of documents. The various guides answer questions on grammar, punctuation, and citations, as well as offer assistance with writing styles and formats for reports, articles, cover letters, and résumés.

Information on Returning to School

Sometimes your best career move is more education.

Comprehensive College Financing Information

htttp://www.infi.net/collegemoney/

This site has information on getting funding for college. Although it is an advertisement for one bank, the information on figuring interest rates and payment schedules is helpful to anyone.

Peterson's Education Center

http://www.petersons.com/

Peterson's is the well-known publisher of guides to colleges. Now the company is taking this information online. This is a great resource for information on undergraduate and graduate programs, as well as summer work, and Peterson's is adding sections on professional training and distance education programs.

Resources for Researching Potential Employers

The indexers and search engines in **Chapter 3** *can also help you locate information in this area.*

Open Market Commercial Sites Index

http://www.directory.net/

This site contains links to over 18,000 commercial organizations on the Internet, and it is expanding daily! You can check the listings alphabetically by company name or search for a list of organizations using keywords to describe their field, industry specialty, or location.

NetSearch (sm)

http://www.ais.net:80/netsearch/

Maintained by American Information Systems, Inc., NetSearch is a fast, searchable database that helps locate companies and resources on the World Wide Web. (Searching by "Employment or Job" produced more than 100 "hits.") To list a company in the NetSearch database, simply click on "Add an entry to the database." Send e-mail to netsearch@ais.net.

Yahoo

http://www.yahoo.com

Yahoo is really one of the most extensive and easy-to-use resources available. Its simple menu leads you deeper into the topics you are interested in, and the keyword search lets you target listings within the site quickly. Use the business resources to begin your search for information.

Government Documents

JobWeb has several links to government documents from its server. You may also want to check out the U.S. Department of Labor at **http://www.dol.gov** *for information on labor regulations, and so on.*

U.S. Government Documents from the University of Missouri, St. Louis

gopher://umslvma.umsl.edu/11/library/govdocs/

This is an absolutely tremendous collection of information for the job hunter provided by the University of Missouri at St. Louis. This Gopher site includes many of the more important reports for job seekers and employers, including

- *Occupational Outlook Handbooks* (all editions 1992–present)
- *Small Business Administration Industry Profiles*
- *Small Business Administration State Profiles*
- *U.S. Census Information* (statistics)
- *U.S. Industrial Outlook–1994* (NTDB version) (statistics)

Library of Congress

http://lcweb.loc.gov/

gopher://marvel.loc.gov/

This is a great starting point for all U.S. government information.

All State Employment Offices by State

ftp://listserv-ftp.dartmouth.edu/pub/listserv/fedjobs/General/stateadr.txt

Found on the **FedJobs** FTP server (*Chapter 9*), this file lists the address and phone number of every state employment office in the United States arranged alphabetically by state.

Information on Relocating

CityNet

http://www.city.net/

CityNet has listings of information and links to servers in over 113 countries. This is a great way to research locations you are considering moving to or places where you have been offered employment.

CityLink

http://www.NeoSoft.com:80/citylink/

CityLink specifically lists cities in the United States. You will find some duplication with CityNet's resources, but it is worth examining both lists.

Employment Directory of American Markets

http://www.careermosaic.com/cm/directory/ed1.html

A publication of Bernard Hodes, Inc., Career Mosaic includes this directory of data on "The Top 50 U.S. Markets," "The Top 10 Canadian Markets," and the Consumer Price Index (CPI) in its Web server. This is a great way to check the availability of talent in a given market and to see what major industries are prevalent there.

Working and Living Overseas

http://www.magi.com/~issi

Put together by Jean-Marc Hachey, author of *The Canadian Guide to Working and Living Overseas*, it says it's a guide for Canadians, but anyone who is considering a move to another country should look this over carefully. It is a clear and concise set of questions and leads for making your move a better one.

Support Groups

Every issue of The National Business Employment Weekly has a list of job-search support groups from around the country with contact information for each. Check your local library or career service center for copies.

Forty Plus of Northern California

http://web.sirius.com/~40plus

Forty Plus of Northern California is a nonprofit self-help group of executives and professionals over 40 who are currently in career transition. There is a fee to use this service. Contact Dr. Jim Moyer (drjimm@sirius.com) for more information.

ABLE~JOB

To Subscribe: listserv@sjuvm.stjohns.edu

Message: subscribe ABLE-JOB yourfirstname yourlastname

This mailing list is dedicated to the advancement of people with disabilities and the workplace experience. Subjects pertaining to research, development, and assistance with online job opportunities for individuals with disabilities are discussed. Suggested topics might include work that can be done at home, companies employing or interested in employing people with disabilities, job development, sources for adaptive technology, disability job-related experiences, job training availability, educational opportunities, discrimination against people with disabilities in the workplace, and the law. The list owners are Dick Banks (rbanks @uwstout.edu) and Robert Ambrose (ambrose@rdz.stjohns.edu). (*See also* ***"Information for the Disabled"*** *in this appendix.*)

alt.support.telecommute

This newsgroup discusses your questions/problems/desires related to pursuing a telecommunications career.

misc.jobs.misc

This newsgroup discusses job hunting. Questions may pertain to a company, that interview you just had, or how to use a recruiter. Please do not post job listings or résumés here.

Information for the Disabled

Resources for Persons with Disabilities from The Catapult

http://www.jobweb.org/CATAPULT/disabled.html

A great collection of links to information resources and employment resources for the disabled, many of these sites include links to legal information, assistive technologies, and support groups, as well as job opportunities.

News You Can Use

The news of the world (and even your little piece of it) can affect how you pursue your job and career options. Usenet newsgroups for specific fields and disciplines can also be a terrific source of current news.

Key Resources for Journalists

http://www.dgsys.com/~editors/resource.html

A part of The Internet Newsroom, this is a source of information for journalists who need help using the Internet.

CNN Online

http://www.cnn.com/

CNN is bringing the idea of late-breaking news to the Internet.

The Omnivore

http://history.cc.ukans.edu/carrie/news_main.html

This comprehensive daily news and information service is housed at the University of Kansas. Major fields covered are business, news, and world reports.

Index of Cited Resources

This index is a quick list of all the resources cited in this book. A full description of each resource is available in the chapter in which it falls. We suggest you begin by reading through the book, noting the resources that interest you, and then use this as a "quick list" to connect to them.

Chapter 2

Career Magazine
http://www.careermag.com/careermag/

CareerMosaic
http://www.careermosaic.com/cm/

Monster Board
http://www.monster.com/

Online Career Center
http://www.occ.com
misc.jobs.resumes

World Wide Job Seekers
http://www.cban.com/resume/

Chapter 3

All of the Gopher Servers in the World (The Mother Gopher)
gopher://gopher.micro.umn.edu:70

Clearinghouse for Subject-Oriented Internet Resource Guides (The Clearinghouse)
http://www.lib.umich.edu/chhome.html

Directory of Academic Discussion Lists (Kovacs List)
http://www.mid.net/KOVACS/

Directory of Electronic Journals, Newsletters, and Academic Discussion Lists
gopher://arl.cni.org (Association of Research Libraries)

Employment Opportunities and Job Resources on the Internet
http://www.wpi.edu/~mfriley/jobguide.html

Galaxy at TradeWave
http://galaxy.einet.net/galaxy.html

Hytelnet 36
http://galaxy.einet.net/hytelnet/HYTELNET.html

Indiana University Mailing List Archive
http://scwww.ucs.indiana.edu/mlarchive/

Jim Milles at the St. Louis University School of Law
http://lawlib.slu.edu/training/mailser.htm

Jughead
gopher://marvel.loc.gov (Library of Congress)

Library of Congress
http://lcweb.loc.gov/

List of All Active Newsgroups
ftp://ftp.uu.net

List of All Usenet Newsgroups
ftp://ftp.uu.net

Master WWW Server List
http://www.w3.org/hypertext/DataSources/WWW/Servers.html

Net-Happenings Archive
http://www.mid.net:80/NET/

Netlink
http://netlink.wlu.edu:1020

NewJour—The Archive of New Electronic Journal Announcements
http://gort.ucsd.edu/newjour/

Newsgroup FAQs
http://www.cis.ohio-state.edu/hypertext/faq/usenet/index.html.

Open Market's Commercial Sites Index
http://www.directory.net/

Publicly-Accessible Mailing Lists (PAML)
http://www.neosoft.com/internet/paml/

RiceInfo
http://riceinfo.rice.edu/RiceInfo/Subject.html

Scholarly Societies Project, University of Waterloo Library
http://www.lib.uwaterloo.ca/society/overview.html

SRI List of Lists
ftp://sri.com

Usenet Newsgroups and Mailing Lists FAQs
http://www.cis.ohio-state.edu/hypertext/faq/usenet/index.html.

Veronica
gopher://gopher.scs.unr.edu:70 (University of Nevada, Reno)

Virtual Library (W3O)
http://www.w3.org/hypertext/DataSources/bySubject/Overview.html

WebCrawler
http://webcrawler.com

Whole Internet Catalogue
http://gnn.com/wic/wics/index.html

WWW Worm
http://www.cs.colorado.edu/wwww/

Yahoo
http://www.yahoo.com/

Chapter 4

America's Job Bank
http://www.ajb.dni.us/

BAMTA, Bay Area Multiple Technology Alliance
http://mlds-www.arc.nasa.gov/form/BAMTA/

biz.jobs.offered

Career Center (from the Internet Professional)
http://www.netline.com/Career/career.html

Career Connections H.E.A.R.T.
http://www.career.com

Career Magazine
http://www.careermag.com/careermag/

Career Web, The Huntington Group
http://www.sgx.com/cw/

Career Web, Landmark Communications
http://www.cweb.com/

CareerMosaic
http://www.careermosaic.com/cm/

Catapult, Career Service Professionals Homepage
http://www.jobweb.org/CATAPULT/catapult.htm

College Grad Job Hunter
http://www.collegegrad.com/

Contract Employment Weekly, Jobs Online
http://www.ceweekly.wa.com/

E-Span, The Interactive Employment Network
http://www.espan.com/

Employment Edge
http://www.employmentedge.com/employment.edge

Employment Opportunities and Job Resources on the Internet (The Riley Guide)
http://www.wpi.edu/~mfriley/jobguide.html

Entry Level Job Seeker Assistant
http://work1.utsi.edu:8000/~jschmalh/jobhome.html

EPages: Jobs Offered Index
http://ep.com/jb.html

GetAJob!!!
http://www.teleport.com/~pcllgn/gaj.html

Harry's Job Search BBS Hot List
http://rescomp.stanford.edu/jobs/jobs-bbs.html

Help Wanted.Com, YSS Inc.
http://www.helpwanted.com/

Help Wanted USA
http://www.webcom.com/~career/hwusa.html

IntelliMatch
http://www.intellimatch.com/

Inter-Links Employment Resources
http://www.nova.edu/Inter-Links/employment.html

Internet Job Locator
http://mtc.globesat.com/jobs/

Internet Professional Association, including the Recruiters OnLine Network
http://www.ipa.com/ipa/

J. Robert Scott
http://j-robert-scott.com/

Job Search and Employment Opportunities: Best Bets from the Net
http://asa.ugl.lib.umich.edu/chdocs/employment/

JobBank USA
http://www.jobbankusa.com/

JobCenter
http://www.jobcenter.com/

JobHunt: A Meta-list of On-Line Job-Search Resources and Services
http://rescomp.stanford.edu/jobs.html

JobNet
http://www.westga.edu/~coop/

Jobs and Career Information
gopher://main.morris.org/11gopher_root%3a5b_jobs%5d

Jobs and Employment
gopher://academic.cc.colorado.edu/11%5b_library._data._jobs%5d

JobTrak
http://www.jobtrak.com

JobWeb
http://www.jobweb.com/

misc.jobs.offered

misc.jobs.offered.entry

Chapter 5

Chapter 6

Chapter 7

Chapter 8

Chapter 9

Chapter 10

Chapter 11

Chapter 12

Halton Community Network
telnet halinet.shericanc.on.ca

Human Resources Development Canada—Metro Toronto
http://www.the-wire.com/hrdc/hrdc.html

ICEN-L — International Career and Employment Network
listserv@IUBVM.UCS.INDIANA.EDU

ie.jobs

iijnet.jobs

Internet Web Recruiting
http://www.internetweb.co.uk/centres/recruitm/recruitm.htm

Irish Job Vacancies Page
http://www.internet-eireann.ie/Ireland/irishjobs.html

JapanNet
http://www.asia-net.com

Jeff Lawrence's Canadian Job Page
http://www.qucis.queensu.ca/home/jlaw/job_stuf.html

Job.net from Computer Contractor
http://www.vnu.co.uk/vnu/cc/

JobSat
jobsat@hookup.net
JobServe
http://www.demon.co.uk/jobserve/

kingston.jobs
kw.jobs

Niagara Peninsula Free-Net
telnet://freenet.niagara.com

ont.jobs

ott.jobs

Overseas Job Net Info Haus Page
http://www.infohaus.com/access/by-seller/Overseas_Job_Net

People Bank
http://www.micromedia.co.uk/ten/

Postdoc International
POST@DOCSERV.SACLAY.CEA.FR

Price Jamieson
http://www.gold.net/PriceJam/

Prince George Free-Net
telnet://freenet.unbc.edu

ProCom
http://www.flexnet.com/flex/procom/homepg.htm

Professionals On Line/Employment and Recruitment
http://www.wordsimages.com/emp_rec.htm

qc.jobs

relcom.commerce.jobs

Russian and East European Institute Employment Opportunities
http://www.indiana.edu/~reeiweb/indemp.html

Singapore Career Opportunities
http://www-leland.stanford.edu/~chongkee/edb/career.html

Span Consultancy
http://www.demon.co.uk/cyberdyne/span/span.html

Student Employment Services, University of Western Ontario
gopher://gopher.uwo.ca:70/11/.services/ses

swnet.jobs

TeleJob
http://ezinfo.ethz.ch/ETH/TELEJOB/tjb_home_e.html

TKO Personnel, Inc
http://www.internet-is.com/tko/

tor.jobs

Toronto Free-Net
telnet://freenet.toronto.on.ca

uk.jobs.d

uk.jobs.offered

uk.jobs.wanted

Vancouver Regional FreeNet
telnet://freenet.vancouver.bc.ca

Victoria Freenet Association (Employment Resources)
gopher://freenet.victoria.bc.ca/11/business

za.ads.jobs

Appendix B

Access America
918-747-2542

Ad Connection
804-978-3927

Advanced R&D's Pipeline
407-894-0580

ALIX
202-707-4885

Analysts International Corporation
214-263-9161

Appendix C

Index

VGM CAREER BOOKS

CAREER DIRECTORIES
Careers Encyclopedia
Dictionary of Occupational Titles
Occupational Outlook Handbook

CAREERS FOR
Animal Lovers
Bookworms
Caring People
Computer Buffs
Crafty People
Culture Lovers
Environmental Types
Fashion Plates
Film Buffs
Foreign Language Aficionados
Good Samaritans
Gourmets
Health Nuts
History Buffs
Kids at Heart
Nature Lovers
Night Owls
Number Crunchers
Plant Lovers
Shutterbugs
Sports Nuts
Travel Buffs
Writers

CAREERS IN
Accounting; Advertising; Business; Child Care; Communications; Computers; Education; Engineering; the Environment; Finance; Government; Health Care; High Tech; International Business; Journalism; Law; Marketing; Medicine; Science; Social & Rehabilitation Services

CAREER PLANNING
Beating Job Burnout
Beginning Entrepreneur
Career Planning & Development for College Students & Recent Graduates
Career Change
Careers Checklists
College and Career Success for Students with Learning Disabilities
Complete Guide to Career Etiquette
Cover Letters They Don't Forget
Dr. Job's Complete Career Guide
Executive Job Search Strategies
Guide to Basic Cover Letter Writing
Guide to Basic Résumé Writing
Guide to Internet Job Searching
Guide to Temporary Employment
Job Interviewing for College Students
Joyce Lain Kennedy's Career Book
Out of Uniform
Slam Dunk Résumés
The Parent's Crash Course in Career Planning: Helping Your College Student Succeed

CAREER PORTRAITS
Animals; Cars; Computers; Electronics; Fashion; Firefighting; Music; Nursing; Sports; Teaching; Travel; Writing

GREAT JOBS FOR
Business Majors
Communications Majors
Engineering Majors
English Majors
Foreign Language Majors
History Majors
Psychology Majors

HOW TO
Apply to American Colleges and Universities
Approach an Advertising Agency and Walk Away with the Job You Want
Be a Super Sitter
Bounce Back Quickly After Losing Your Job
Change Your Career
Choose the Right Career
Cómo escribir un currículum vitae en inglés que tenga éxito
Find Your New Career Upon Retirement
Get & Keep Your First Job
Get Hired Today
Get into the Right Business School
Get into the Right Law School
Get into the Right Medical School
Get People to Do Things Your Way
Have a Winning Job Interview
Hit the Ground Running in Your New Job
Hold It All Together When You've Lost Your Job
Improve Your Study Skills
Jumpstart a Stalled Career
Land a Better Job
Launch Your Career in TV News
Make the Right Career Moves
Market Your College Degree
Move from College into a Secure Job
Negotiate the Raise You Deserve
Prepare Your Curriculum Vitae
Prepare for College
Run Your Own Home Business
Succeed in Advertising When all You Have Is Talent
Succeed in College
Succeed in High School
Take Charge of Your Child's Early Education
Write a Winning Résumé
Write Successful Cover Letters
Write Term Papers & Reports
Write Your College Application Essa

MADE EASY
Cover Letters
Getting a Raise
Job Hunting
Job Interviews
Résumés

OPPORTUNITIES IN
This extensive series provides detailed information on nearly 150 individual career fields.

RÉSUMÉS FOR
Advertising Careers
Architecture and Related Careers
Banking and Financial Careers
Business Management Careers
College Students & Recent Graduates
Communications Careers
Education Careers
Engineering Careers
Environmental Careers
Ex-Military Personnel
50+ Job Hunters
Government Careers
Health and Medical Careers
High School Graduates
High Tech Careers
Law Careers
Midcareer Job Changes
Re-Entering the Job Market
Sales and Marketing Careers
Scientific and Technical Careers
Social Service Careers
The First-Time Job Hunter

VGM Career Horizons
a division of *NTC Publishing Group*
4255 West Touhy Avenue
Lincolnwood, Illinois 60646–1975